Through It All

PSALM 37:4

By Albert Garcia

Through It ALL
A Story Of God's Redemptive Power, Mercy, And Grace

© 2021 Albert Garcia

ISBN: 978-0-9966317-8-5

For information, please contact
allbertgarcia6719@gmail.com

Worlds of Wonder
BOOKS • VIDEO • WEB

Cover Design Tim Cocklin
www.worldsofwonderpublishing.com

Through It All

By Albert Garcia

In Memory

This book is dedicated to the memory of my beloved son John Michael Garcia. Not a day goes by that I don't think about you, son. I love and miss you. Love, Dad

Dedication

I dedicate this book to my Lord and Savior, Jesus Christ. I thank God for being there for me when I hadn't a clue about Him. He knew me before I was even born. It was God who wrote my story. May He receive all the glory for this book.

I also would like to dedicate this book to my children, grandchildren, and future generations not born yet. The most important decision you can make is to decide to follow Jesus. My prayer for each of you is that you will know that God loves you.

Acknowledgements

Many people have been a part of helping these pages come to be.

First, and foremost I would like to give many thanks to my beautiful wife, Natasha, for her endless hours of making this book come to life.

I want to thank my son, Andrew, for all his help with the stories. Even when you were busy with your studies, you helped. Thank you, son.

I want to thank my kids, Brandi, Albert, and Anthony. Thank you for allowing me to talk about you in the book. Thank you for loving me.

I also want to thank my stepdaughters, Jennifer & Jessica. You are both just as daughters to me. Thank you for allowing me to talk about your mom in the book.

I wish to thank Jennifer Chavez and Carisa Segovia for their insightful help with this book. I am so very grateful for all your knowledge.

This book wouldn't be possible without the knowledge and wisdom of Tim Cocklin. Thank you for helping to make the book a reality. I thank God for Him directing me to you.

I want to thank my Pastor, Marty Burroughs, for being the one who finally persuaded me give my testimony in front of an audience. It was a necessary step for this book to be written. Thank you for faithfully leading us each Sunday morning.

I want to thank my mother, Manchita (Irma) for being a good mom. Thank you to each of my sisters; Leticia, Diana, Alicia, Yolanda, and Olga. A special thanks to my brother Hector and his wife, Lori, who helped with one of the stories.

Finally, I would like to thank my fellow officer's that I worked with on the force. Thanks to my old partner, Rick Sepolio, Sr; though no longer here, he left me with much wisdom.

My wife Natasha and I were on vacation in Branson, Missouri when she saw this sign with a giant penny in front of a shop. Intrigued by the penny, we knew we had to enter the store. Susan wasn't at the shop on our first visit. The following year we returned to the shop for a second visit. That's where we met the store owner, Susan Abar. She shared her powerful

testimony with us. Before we left the store, we purchased her book, along with many other goodies. In her book, Susan shares about her occurrences with copper pennies. Since then, she has become a good friend of ours. She was a blessing by referring author and publisher Tim Cocklin to us. It was no coincidence that we visited The Copper Coin. I believe that the Lord led us there. If you are ever in Branson, stop by her shop. Thank you, Susan.

Contents

Jeremiah 29:11

For I know the plans I have for you," declares the LORD, "plans to prosper you and not to harm you, plans to give you hope and a future.

Prologue

It was a Saturday afternoon, and I was looking forward to my shift because it was my Friday. My regular days off were Sundays and Mondays. As a police officer, you don't get a lot of time to spend with your family. When you're at work, you are entirely engaged in the task at hand because if you're not, it could be the difference between life and death. Your time off is precious because it might be another five days before you would spend any meaningful time with your family. I was looking forward to the coming Sunday; we planned to go to church and have lunch together.

As I walked into the station, I remember being in a joyful mood. It was a beautiful, cool crisp January day. I went straight to the roll call room, where all the officers were gathered. The atmosphere was buzzing as everyone seemed to be ready to head out to the streets. The evening shift was usually the most active. I worked with some great officers in Kingwood, men I knew I could trust to have my back.

I hadn't been at the station long before the evening Sergeant waved me into his office. It was unusual but not worrisome. I assumed it wasn't anything serious, that maybe I needed to sign some paperwork. Once in his office, he asked me to take a seat, and I jokingly said, "Is someone complaining about me? That's ok; I don't need to sit. What's up, Sarge?" I could see it in his face and hear it in his voice; he was not joking. He was serious. He stood up to close the door behind me. His expression told me that it might not be good, so when he motioned to the chair and said, "Have a seat," I did as he asked.

1

Brownsville

On July 29, 1955, I came into this world at my grandmother's home in Brownsville, Texas, with the help of a midwife. Brownsville is located in South Texas and is commonly referred to as the Rio Grande Valley. It is within walking distance from the United States International Bridge that crosses into Matamoros, Mexico. In 1955, most of the quiet border town's residents were Mexican Americans, or *Chicanos*. In those days, almost everyone knew each other. Your neighbor knew his neighbor's business, and everything that happened spread around town. A person's past was hard to escape. It was even more challenging for someone to turn his or her life around. But that didn't stop people from trying.

My father, Adalberto Hernandez Garcia, was born in Brownsville, Texas and my mother, Irma Montez Garcia was born in San Benito, Texas. Most *Chicanos* called this region *El Valle* (The Valley). My parents could trace their lineage back to when Texas was known as *Tejas*. My dad worked through blood, sweat, and tears for everything we had, which wasn't very much. Despite having very little, we always had food on the table. I was the oldest of my seven siblings, five sisters and two brothers. We were a close family, who loved one another, but the word itself was never actually spoken. We didn't talk about it but we knew that we loved one another.

My father was a tough man who never showed much emotion towards us. I don't remember him showing much affection towards my mother, either. I'm not sure he knew how. But sure enough, they had a lot of kids. He'd lived a tough life growing up in *El Valle*, shaped by poverty and lack of education. In his teenage years, he was what in those days would be called a *pachuco* or gangster, who ran the streets with a neighborhood gang called *La Parra*. He made some wrong choices and got involved in his fair share of dangerous situations. He found himself on the wrong side of the law in Brownsville. Without going into details, let's just say he led a dangerous lifestyle. However, my father gave up that *pachuco* lifestyle when his children came into the picture. He was not very affectionate, but he showed his love in other ways. We always had a roof over our heads, even though we never stayed in the same place for long.

My mother was and still is a beautiful woman with long wavy hair and light green eyes from her father's side of the family, which originated from Spain. She endured many hard times growing up with a single mother. Life was not kind to her, but she made the best of it. She was kind and gentle when caring for us. Showing affection with words didn't come naturally for my mom, either. She didn't have that warmth demonstrated to her growing up. Her mother had issues with men, and often, she had to fend for herself. But we knew she loved us by how much she cared for us. It was a tough job, but we were always bathed, clothed, and fed.

My parents were poor. Throughout the years, they regularly traveled to other states in search of work for my dad. They didn't have much education to lean on for help. Both of my parents dropped out of school well before graduating high school. My dad's education ended in the ninth grade, and my mom's even sooner. My parents spoke primarily Spanish at home, with English being their second language.

My mom was only thirteen when she married my father, who was nineteen. They met while my mom was still in school. He would see her walking to school and would flirt and whistle as she passed by. He was older and intriguing, with his black hair slicked back, and eventually, they began talking. By law, my grandmother, Herminia De Los Santos, had to sign off for them to get married. Marrying young wasn't uncommon in those days. It was common for Mexican American women and women of all cultures to be *stay-at-home moms* while the husband worked.

My mother had her first child at the age of fourteen years old. My dad was a musician and spent many late nights playing gigs. I imagine it must have been a bit lonely, but my mother never complained. She was too busy having to take care of us. Looking back, we were blessed to have such a good mother.

I have memories of my childhood during the '60s. I remember when I was about eight years old while going to grammar school in Brownsville. At school, the mornings would begin with the teacher and the students reciting The Pledge of Allegiance. That was the first time hearing the words *"One Nation under GOD!"* Right after that, the class would have a moment of prayer. That stuck with me, even though my life choices wouldn't reflect that for quite some time. Our parents never spoke to us about God, nor was the name of Jesus ever mentioned. We never attended church or knew how to pray. We didn't know what we were missing. If it weren't for my great-grandmother, Maria, I wouldn't have ever stepped foot in a church as a child.

My great-grandmother, Maria Hernandez Rodriguez, raised my father and his brother, Nayo. She lived alone for many years in Brownsville. I have a fond memory of her, which is embedded in my heart till this very day. Maria took me to church when I was nine or ten years old. One day, I had spent the night at her house; Maria woke me up and told me, "Get ready, you're going to church." She was a devout Catholic. Going to church, I recall her wearing a black veil covering her head, with a rosary in her hand. While inside the cathedral, I felt a sense of peaceful quietness. It was utterly silent inside the church. By the entrance, we stopped at a small fountain where she dipped my finger in the water and showed me how to make the sign of the cross, from forehead to chest, and then shoulder to shoulder. Inside, I remember seeing several religious statues as we paused to light a candle. She softly explained to me that the figures were symbols of God's saints. In the middle of the sanctuary, a large image of a man hung on a cross. I had no idea who He was or why He was up there, and I was too afraid to break the silence by asking.

At her small home, Maria kept a religious shrine with lit candles, which surrounded a *Virgin Mary* figurine. She also had a picture of that man on the cross I had seen at church. She told me His name was Jesus and what He had done for us. I am grateful for the memory that my great-grandmother placed in me. She was the first person who told me about the Lord, but I was too young to understand.

Years later, after Maria's death, I discovered that she held deep secrets from her past. My aunt, Concepcion, shared a story about Maria. In the 20th century, Maria was involved in the *Mexican Revolution* with Francisco Villa's army, who opposed the government's corrupted rule. According to my aunt, during Maria's youth, the Mexican Soldados (*Soldiers*) had killed her husband, who was a train conductor. Because of this, Maria resented the Mexican government and wished to see it fall. Along with other women, Maria assisted in helping Villa's army by delivering guns concealed in wagons.

She believed in the cause that Francisco Villa was advocating for the poor farmers.

Consequently, at the end of the Mexican revolution Francisco Villa, known as *Pancho Villa,* was assassinated, resulting in many of his poor supporters immigrating to the United States. So, Maria and her daughter (my dad's mother) settled in Brownsville, Texas, in the late 1920s. My aunt Concepcion said that Maria lived in fear and seldom spoke about her past. Maria was buried in Brownsville, Texas, and was over 100 years old at her death.

Elgin, Illinois

In 1962 we lived in Elgin, Illinois. I was seven years old, and my sister, Leticia (Letty), was five. I remember us having to walk several blocks to get to school, which was on the other side of the train tracks. Sometimes, the snow got very thick during the winter. One day, while walking to school, the train had come to a complete stop, blocking our access to cross the street. We were unable to pass, and I wanted to make it to school in time, so I decided to be a bit adventurous and climbed up inside one of the boxcars. As I motioned for Letty to get on board, the train suddenly jolted and slowly started to move. My sister got scared that I would be taken away and started crying. I, too, was frightened and immediately jumped out, tumbling to the ground. After brushing myself off, I remember instructing Letty not to tell my parents what had happened. My father would have indeed given me a spanking.

At the time, my two younger sisters, Diana and Alicia, were too young to attend school. Our dad worked at a factory in Elgin, and our mother had recently given birth to our baby brother Dario. Sadly, baby Dario did not live long. He became sick of pneumonia and died at the hospital. At that time, medicine was not as advanced as it is now. He was only three months old when he passed away. We didn't understand why this happened, and my parents did not speak much about it. My dad grieved in private. We never saw him cry. My mom was sad but kept on taking care of us as usual.

It wasn't until I was an adult that my mother talked about the day Dario died. She said the doctor walked over to my father and her and gave them the terrible news, and he allowed them to hold my baby brother's lifeless body. My mother cried and mourned for the loss of her son. But it was what my mother told me about my father that has always struck me. She spoke of my dad, grabbing Dario's lifeless body and holding him against his chest, shouting, *"Mijo, Mijo!" Son, Son!* He wept out loud in deep sorrow; she said she had never seen my dad cry before that day. My parents buried Dario in Elgin, Illinois. The thought of my dad weeping over my little brother still saddens me today. It illustrated a vulnerable side of my dad that I appreciated my mom sharing with me.

Not long after my brother's death, our parents decided to return to Texas, where we lived temporarily at my grandmother Herminia's house in Brownsville.

Our mother would re-register Letty and me back into the Brownsville School District, and we did our best to continue with life. But there was always a sense of emptiness left by Dario's absence. By this time, my mother was pregnant with my younger brother Hector, and my dad had gone to find work in San Antonio. Once he had a job and got settled in, he returned for us. By the time he returned to Brownsville, my brother Hector had been born. Life seemed to return to normal, as my mom was busy caring for my new brother.

3

Moving to Cali

In 1965, my aunt Elva and uncle Robert visited our family in Brownsville. They had lived in Watsonville, California, for many years. Their two kids, both teenagers at the time, did not make the trip with them to Texas.

Each time they came into town, my siblings and I would wait in suspense to see what car they would be driving. Every time we saw them, they were in a brand new vehicle. My family and I would joke and say, "I wonder what car they are driving this time." I remember thinking it must be nice to have that much money. During every visit, they would attempt to persuade my parents to move to California. They'd boast about all the opportunities in agriculture and the canneries.

They finally succeeded in their attempt to get my family to leave. My parents decided to follow work, and we started packing for our move to California. My aunt and uncle had a job lined up for my dad picking apples.

We didn't own a vehicle at the time, so my aunt suggested we ride in their new camper truck. I was ten years old, crammed into the truck's bed with my parents, sisters Leticia, Alicia, Yolanda, and little brother Hector. Our sister

Diana stayed behind with an aunt in Brownsville. At the time, she was only six years old. Our little sister Olga had not been born yet.

I don't remember too much of our road trip to California, but I recollect it being cold. As we crossed the state line, my eyes filled with excitement at the snow-covered mountains. They were the California Sierra Mountains. It was quite a different view from our home in Brownsville. The last time I saw snow was in Illinois.

When we reached Watsonville, we stayed with our aunt and uncle until our parents could rent a house. It wasn't long before we moved into a little place upon a hilltop, overlooking the valley below.

My brother Hector and I had a lot of fun playing on top of that hill. It was an enchanting place. The majestic trees were just yards from our quaint, wooden house. We used to climb up one of those trees to reach an old rugged tree house that looked like it had been there forever.

On the hillside were remnants of two old cars that appeared to have been swallowed by a giant crater, likely resulting from an earthquake. We loved excavating small tunnels while playing inside the massive hole. We'd imagine the magical places they would take us to. We'd venture in a little, but not too far for fear that the tunnel would cave in on top of us.

I remember the beautiful Santa Cruz Valley landscape that overlooked colorful vineyards and orchards. I spent hours, upon hours outdoors. One of my favorite things to do was to enjoy the peaceful sights, sounds, and smells of nature.

Another favored activity of Hector's and mine was surfing down the dry, grassy slopes of the hilltop on large cardboard pieces, tumbling to the ground in the end. We'd stay out, sliding down over and over until the sun began to drop below the horizon. We could hear our mother's voice in the distance yelling for us to come home for dinner, just like on the show *Little House on a Prairie*.

It wasn't all fun and outdoor adventures. As soon as we unpacked and were situated, my mother registered Letty and me in school. My other siblings were still too young to attend school. In the chilly, misty mornings, the bus driver would blow the horn, and Letty and I would race down the hill. I didn't mind riding the bus. There were lots of pleasant sights to take in during the drive to school.

Living in California was a happy time for us. I enjoyed going to school. I had many friends, and I liked my teacher. I was excited to learn and loved doing the projects. My enthusiasm showed on my report card in the form of excellent grades.

My mother made sure my sister and I were always clean to go to school. I remember her washing our clothes by hand in a large galvanized tub. Thinking back, I guess you can say we were the Mexican American *hillbillies* of California. To top it off, we even had an outhouse for a restroom.

Our time in California was probably my favorite time growing up. But as was typical with my family, we didn't stay long. We lived there for only a short time before we moved back to Texas. I was sad to leave the beauty of our hilltop to go back to Brownsville's flat, dry landscape; however, with as much as my family moved, I knew it was a possibility that we'd be back.

Tepee

In 1968, we moved to San Antonio, Texas, for the second time. We had lived there once before in 1965 for a short while. And as usual, my siblings and I started a new school in the middle of a semester. At the time, my dad was working at a food-processing factory. On the weekends, he played his accordion in a *Tejano* band. I later realized that my dad didn't keep a job long due to his drinking and the late nights spent playing in the clubs.

San Antonio had a large *Chicano* population in the sixties. It was known for hard-core *pachucos* or neighborhood gangs. Most of the friends that my dad had were *pachucos*.

We lived in the San Pedro district off Euclid Avenue in an upstairs fourplex home. I remember the house was an old-style colonial home with large columns facing towards the street. I was thirteen years old. From our upstairs apartment window, you could see the Tower of the Americas (also known as the Hemisphere). During the Tower's grand opening celebration, our class went on a field trip to observe the festivities. I often have moments when I remember this time of life in San Antonio.

My siblings and I experienced the most significant, unforgettable occurrence in San Antonio; we fell in love with the downstairs neighbor's dog. The owners were two teenage gangsters who had too much time on their hands and sadly cruelty in their hearts. Tepee was always tied up outside. It was evident how bad the teenagers treated the dog by the scar marks on his hind legs, all because they kept him tied up with clothing wire.

At times, my siblings and I would feed Tepee, who always appeared to be hungry. By looking at his frame, it was evident that he hadn't eaten in days. The two young delinquents hated that my siblings and I would feed their dog. They chased us away with the threat of harsh profanities and promises of hurt. They intimidated us, as they were much older. Meanwhile, my dad developed a soft spot for Tepee.

There were several times when Tepee managed to get loose, and he immediately ran upstairs to our unit. Usually, he would be waiting for us by our front door after school. Soon after, both teenagers would show up at our front door knocking, and we had no choice but to release Tepee back to their care. They would drag him back to his usual spot.

In those days, there were no laws regarding cruelty to animals.

One day, after an incident of Tepee escaping, the teenage delinquents were cussing and threatening us. This time, our dad overheard them. I remember my dad shouting back at them and telling them, "Feed the poor dog, and maybe he won't run away." After that, I think they had it in for us. But my dad wasn't scared of anything or anyone. I do believe he was concerned about our safety. He suspected the gangsters would try to retaliate. I remember feeling the hostility while living there. Not long after, our parents decided to move to a house down the street, and somehow Tepee knew how to track us down. There were times that he would occasionally show up at our front door. It wasn't long before Tepee's owners would find out where we lived and came to retrieve him.

During one of Tepee's bold escapes, both guys showed up and began violently banging at our door. My dad quickly answered, and an argument ensued. The bullies were yelling and cussing at my dad, wanting to know where the dog was. My dad shouted back in Spanish, "The dog is staying!" I remember one thug screamed, "Come outside, and we'll see about that!" Honestly, I think my dad had enough of them threatening his family. I remember seeing my dad step outside and waved at both of them to *bring it on.* It made me proud to see my dad stand up to these guys.

After seeing that my dad showed no fear, they slowly backed off and walked away. They never bothered us again, and Tepee became our first pet.

After one year of living in San Antonio, our dad informed us that we would move to Houston. I remember it was a Friday evening; I had just gotten home from school when my dad said we were moving the next day. *Talk about short notice!* Our dad informed us that his cousin in Houston had a job waiting for him. I was tired of hearing the words "we are moving." My heart sank. I had recently been promoted as a student crossing guard at school and had just completed my first week. I enjoyed that school assignment and finally felt as if I belonged there.

Sadly we moved, without saying goodbye to my school friends. It had always been like that growing up with my parents continually moving. We couldn't say much since we were young.

The next night, which was on a Saturday, a *pachuco* friend of our fathers was on his way to pick us up. He was going to drive us to Houston. My dad had a car, but I don't remember what happened to it. He could have very well sold it for the trip and to get us a place to live in Houston.

We asked my parents, "What about Tepee?" They got quiet, and then my dad explained that Tepee wasn't going.

He said that there was only a small amount of room and that his friend did not want a dog in the car.

My siblings and I were so hurt when we heard that Tepee was staying. We had come to love the little dog. We were heartbroken.

"Let's go," said my parents as they advised us to help load just the immediate necessities for the trip. I remember Tepee trailing behind us, and he was probably wondering, what was going on.

The next thing you know, we are all crammed up in the back seat, with my dad seated up front, talking to his friend as we pulled out onto the street. My siblings and I kept looking out the back window at Tepee.

My little brother Hector, my sisters, and I observed poor Tepee following behind the car as it started to pull out of the driveway. My sister Letty started weeping and saying, "Papi, we see Tepee following behind." Next thing I realized, the car was accelerating, and we were on the freeway ramp. We had never seen Tepee run so fast, his scarred little legs desperately trying to catch up with us. When we saw Tepee slow to a stop, my brother and I burst out crying. Even our mother started crying.

Seeing us cry must have moved our dad's heart. I guess he understood the poor dog had had it rough, and we were abandoning him. But I honestly believe our *tough-guy* dad couldn't bear to see his children cry.

At that very moment, I heard my dad say in Spanish, "Pull over, and let's get the dog." His friend said, "No, Beto! We are already on the freeway." In a stern voice, my dad looked at him and said, "Let's go back and get the dog, or we are not going!"

Sure enough, we exited the freeway and returned to the house. I remember the headlights of the car beaming at the home and seeing Tepee sitting by the door. As soon as

Tepee saw us, he jumped inside the vehicle with us, and off we went to Houston.

5

Houston

After moving to Houston from San Antonio in 1968, we settled in the Montrose area, which is several blocks west of downtown Houston. We lived in a duplex house on the corner of Fairview and Mason Street. During this time, the community had many longhaired hippies who hosted boisterous outdoor block parties every week. Most of the landlords were Caucasians, who kindly rented their houses to Chicanos. The area was well known for the numerous Honky Tonk bars. As a kid, I had never seen a cowboy, especially from the places we traveled with our parents. The only recollection I had about cowboys came from the black and white western shows such as Bonanza and The Lone Ranger. They showed how the cowboys would dress in their western clothing. The Montrose was definitely multi-cultural during the early seventies.

Life was fun in Houston. I had made many friends who were my age. I enjoyed hanging out with the neighborhood kids, and we would ride our bikes as far as to the Astrodome. We loved playing cops and robbers while chasing each other on our bicycles. I smile at the memory of one of my friends; he always wanted to play the policeman because he could make an excellent siren noise, while I would play the robber, making the big getaway as he chased me around the neighborhood.

One day, a friend and I purchased two shoeshine boxes, and we started going into the Honky Tonk beer joints to make money polishing cowboy boots. We quickly learned the trade, and we charged seventy-five cents per shine. The best days for the job were Friday and Saturday nights. I remember the tall western-dressed cowboys would throw in an extra quarter for a tip. We were fifteen years old, and the profits were significant. Soon after, my friend and I would rush to the mom-and-pop store to buy candy, chips, and soda pops. The cowboys never bothered us, nor did we ever feel threatened. They just wanted their boots looking nice and polished as they stood leaning against the bar listening to country music playing on the jukebox. I even began to enjoy hearing Patsy Cline and Hank William's songs.

My neighborhood friends and I would play hooky from school. We roamed the Houston streets, killing time playing football and walking around. Although one day, my friends got busted by their parents, and they stopped missing school. There were times I skipped school alone and would hang out inside a payphone booth. I would pretend I was talking on the phone with someone, so no one would be suspicious of why I wasn't in school. By this time, I had learned to dislike school. Honestly, I hated it! I was registered at Lanier Junior High, whose mascot was the Purple Pups. Unfortunately, the grades on my report card were straight D's and F's. I blamed it on switching so many schools while growing up. On top of that, I had fallen behind on a grade or two. *Imagine that!*

It wasn't long before the truancy officer knocked at our door and asked my mother why I wasn't in school. After finding out that I had been skipping school, my mother was very angry with me, but she never told my father. My mother knew the harsh discipline he would have given me as an example to my siblings.

6

My Dad's Band

Much like the places we lived before, my father played in a Tejano band once we moved to Houston. One day the drummer up and quit, and they needed a drummer urgently. They had a show that night and were desperately looking for someone to play. I was fifteen years old, and I already knew how to play the drums from the lessons I learned growing up. My father taught me to play on a few tin cans. However, he was reluctant for me to join the group out of concern for my safety. I believe he didn't want me to spend any time at the clubs he performed in. But considering the band's critical situation and that I was on summer break from school, he allowed it. That weekend, I became his new drummer.

While playing in the band with my father, there were times when fights would break out in the Mexican cantinas. My dad would always tell me to hide low behind my drum-set, as sometimes beer bottles became flying projectiles.

During the early seventies, I earned fifty to sixty dollars a night for a four-hour performance, which wasn't bad for a teenager in a four-person band. I would give half of my earnings to my mom to help with the bills. I would spend my money on clothes, expensive haircuts, and brand new shoes, with money left over to see a picture show. Girls weren't in the picture yet. There were older girls in the clubs, but I was still a kid, and those thoughts never crossed my mind.

I will always have those cherished memories of playing in the band with my dad. He was strict on discipline, which kept me safe in the clubs. Looking back, I'm thankful for him being strict. He kept me walking the straight line. He didn't want me to take the same route that he did.

California Summer

After living in Houston for almost 3 years, our father had the urge to move *again* and suggested we relocate to Elgin, Illinois, where we had once lived.

I often wondered if my dad got the urge to move because he was trying to avoid outstanding traffic warrants or was possibly in trouble with the law. My parents always claimed it was because my dad was in search of a job. Even with all the changes and shuffling us around, one thing remained constant; my dad always had his accordion with him wherever he went. It was his most prized possession throughout the years and a means of earning money in a pinch.

When my dad wanted to move to Elgin, my siblings and I were already teenagers and tired of our lives being turned upside down. Being the oldest, I argued and pleaded with our parents to stay in Houston. I had friends, income, and a life. My sisters also begged them for us to stay. After seeing his opinionated kids were not children anymore, he decided that Houston would be our hometown. However, we ended up taking off to California for the summer to earn money during the harvest picking. When our parents agreed to make Houston our home, we all squealed in delight. Even my father cracked a smile.

In 1971, we returned to California for a second time. By this time, my sister Diana, who we called Didi, lived with my aunt permanently, so she didn't make the trip with us. There were many things we missed out on with our sister. Reflecting back, one positive thing was that she was the only one of my siblings that graduated from high school.

It wasn't tunnels and cardboard surfing this time in Cali. Now, I was sixteen and was part of my dad's band. We performed gigs on the weekends. During the week, I was expected to help with family responsibilities, such as household chores. My dad made sure I kept my nose out of trouble. The one thing he always told me was, "do what I tell you, not what I do."

The school was out for the summer, so my siblings and I would occasionally help my dad pick apples and onions. At first, it seemed easy and fun; however, it took quite a toll on the body after working many hours under the California sun, especially for a kid.

I remember my dad working in the apple orchards. You would see rows and rows of apple trees as far as the eye could see. While out in the fields, the apples were not edible because of the harmful pesticides that were used. We would take a few apples home and rinse them off heartily before snacking on them.

My siblings and I would help our dad fill a large four-by-four-foot wooden crate with apples gathered from the fields. The earnings weren't that great, at only $9.00 per container. It typically took about three or four apple trees to fill each bin.

It wasn't all hard work, though. I did enjoy horsing around in the orchards' peaceful grounds. I would climb trees and drop apples down to the rich California soil. My siblings' job was to gather the apples from the ground and place them in the crates.

One day, Hector and I were playing war, throwing apples at each other. I was up in a tree and had a clear sight of Hector's noggin below. So, I grabbed a large apple and aimed it at the top of his head...*BOMB'S AWAY! Bull's-eye!* I hit my target, right smack in the middle of my brother's head.

His piercing screams could be heard throughout the orchards. I burst out laughing, thinking it was hilarious; however, my dad disagreed. As he rushed to Hector's aid and saw me laughing up in the tree, he began cursing at me in Spanish. He was grabbing apples from the ground and hurling them, trying to whack me with them. Boy, I wasn't laughing as I dodged the apples. I was scared. I was in deep trouble and too afraid to climb down. Eventually, I had no choice but to come down and accept my fate. As soon as we got home, my dad gave me some grade-A corporal punishment. He never spared the rod! After the incident, my dad never again allowed us to help him at work.

On Friday and Saturday nights, I would perform with my dad's band. I enjoyed playing the drums. We played at many cantinas in Watsonville, San Jose, and Salinas. The money was good, and the work was a lot easier than picking crops. We basically were getting paid for making people dance. We would also earn quite a bit in tips from patrons requesting particular songs. My father always made sure that my mom received money to pay the bills and half of my earnings.

As a frequent reminder, my dad would always make a point to tell me of the dangers and violence that could occur in the places we would perform. In other words, the places we performed weren't an elegant dance hall. The halls were dark with minimal lighting and were breeding grounds for trouble.

I can say, without a doubt, he was right. The cantinas were no place for a teenager. I witnessed gang fights, stabbings, and shootings. My father always taught me to stay alert. Later, as an adult, I understood what he meant. It was about intuition, survival in the hood!

At that time, in California, the Chicano movement was prevalent. Bars and cantinas were packed with pachucos, some of which were fresh out of prison, sporting their tattoos. They spoke a specific chuco dialect. From hearing my father and his friend's conversations, I understood what they were saying in their chuco lingo. They seemed to be trying to show off their *machismo*. Some, in particular, were looking for a rumble, and their weapon of choice was the knife.

In most of the cantinas we played, I noticed most patrons were serious about respecting the Golden Rule. No one messed with the musicos (musicians), or the party would be over. And that meant no more *Baile La Bamba*. There were occasions when a pachuco's girl would be flirting with the musician, and before you knew it, a fight would break out with the band. It went with the territory. We really had to stay on guard, looking out for flying fists and beer bottles.

Looking back at my dad's character, I can acknowledge the influence he had on me. He was always a quiet man who was never an instigator. But he was also not afraid to stand up against a troublemaker. As a kid, I saw him handle himself well in a few fights. He was strong and brave when he needed to be and cautious when his involvement wasn't necessary. I know his streetwise views kept us safe many times. I know now that God had protected us as well! I'm thankful for both my earthly father and my Heavenly Father.

Drop-Out

When we returned to Houston from California, I noticed a lot had changed in the neighborhood. Some of my childhood friends were using drugs. I discovered that a few of them had been locked up in reform school. Once they were released, some of them had a hardened attitude. Many of my old neighborhood friends became involved in gang activity. Most of the gang fights were only fist fights; guns were not involved. My friends were not the same kids I once knew.

As I look back now, I thank God for His hand on my life. I couldn't see it then, but it's obvious now that I was protected by God's grace, something I knew nothing about at the time. I'm also grateful that my dad kept me away from the hood, but he couldn't keep me from making my own bad decisions.

One day after school, my dad got a hold of my report card, which was terrible news for me. It was full of failing grades and evidence of low attendance. However, I did have excellent conduct.

Angry and upset, the next morning, he decided to personally drive me to school. Looking back, it seems as if it were yesterday. I remember that drive; we didn't live far from there, but it felt like an eternity as he lectured me about the importance of staying in school. He expressed his regret that he and my mother had never finished school; he entailed what that had meant for us as a family. He wanted a better future for me. I didn't dare to tell him that maybe we shouldn't have moved so much, for I respected my father. But that is precisely what I felt in my heart.

I remember exiting the car and strolling towards the building. As I got closer to the doors, a nervous rush came over my whole body. I glanced back at my dad; his eyes were steady, staring at me, making sure I walked inside the school.

I reminded myself that I had my excuse note from my mom, as it had become a regular routine with my absences from school. Once inside, the quiet hallways were empty; the students were in class. Instantly, disturbing and embarrassing thoughts raced through my mind. I would have to face the teacher and students who hardly knew me because of my lousy attendance. I wondered how I could get out of that situation. Both my thoughts and heart were racing. I felt my feet begin to move in the opposite direction from class. They knew my mind before I did. I was going to bail. I quickly headed for the back door, hoping no one would see me.

Finally, I made it outside; the celebration of freedom came over me. I thought to myself, *I did it; I'm out of here!* I even forgot about my dad. I picked up the pace along the public sidewalk, trying to put as much distance between the school and me as I could. My celebration ended abruptly as my dad drove up next to the curb, yelling obscenities in Spanish and English. He screamed at me, "get inside the car!" *Oh, man. I was in so much trouble.*

After scolding me, he told me that I needed to get a job if I would not go to school. That actually relieved me. *Anything! Just get me out of that place!*

That's when my education came to an end. I was an eighth-grade dropout. At the time, I was relieved and excited not to have to return to school. It wouldn't be until I was an adult that I would feel the effects of not finishing school. If I could go back, I would have tried harder to complete school. I believe moving to so many different places impacted my poor education. Later as an adult, I promised myself that I would never do that to my children.

Boy's Town

Growing up, I was a shy, skinny kid with long hair. By the age of sixteen, girls were not a part of the picture yet. I had always been bashful with girls and never knew how to approach or even have a conversation with them. My father made an awkward attempt to ask me if I had ever been sexually involved with a girl; he questioned if I liked girls. I believe he mistook my innocence for possibly being gay. I told him that I did very much so like girls but never had sex before. So, my dad suggested that it was time for me to *man-up*.

One day, we traveled to the valley in Brownsville, and we drove across the international bridge into Matamoros, Mexico. My dad had explained that we were going to a place known as *La Sona Roja* (The Red Light District), where legal prostitution was permitted.

I remember that hot summer night as we parked our car and walked the dirt roads leading to the cantinas. The brothels were inside the cantinas. I was excited, but nervousness began to kick in with a sense of shyness, naïve about what I would experience. My father had explained that I was going to be with a woman. When we got near the red light district, you could hear the sounds of live bands playing Mexican music.

On each side of the street, you could see the women standing outside waiting for customers as they stood by the cantina's doors. You could hear them whistling at us and saying in Spanish, "young boy pick me; pick me!" I assumed they already knew why I was there with my father. I observed women of all ages.

Upon entering one of the cantinas, I could see the women, partially dressed, standing along the bar, waiting for someone to pick them.

As I stood there mesmerized, too many to choose from, I heard my dad say, "Pick one, pick the one you want!" So, I did as I was told. That night, I had my first sexual experience with a prostitute.

On the drive home back to Houston, there was not much conversation about what had occurred. As I said before, my dad was a man of few words. I guess he was proud that his oldest son had become what he believed was *a man*. I suppose one could say he meant well with what his life experiences had taught him, but it also goes without saying that it caused me more harm than good.

Indeed, it was there in Boy's Town where the seeds of sexual and lustful desires were conceived. Later in life, it became an obsession of having sex with women. In time, it turned into an addiction, resulting in me not knowing how to have a healthy, monogamous relationship. I saw women as objects. I became full of lust for women.

James 1:15 (NIV) Then, after desire has conceived, it gives birth to sin; and sin, when it is full-grown, gives birth to death.

10

Delivery Driver

I was eighteen years old when I got my driver's license. I started working my first full-time job delivering flowers for Miss Polly's Flower Shop. It was located in the affluent River Oaks area on the west side of Houston. Miss Polly was a kind, elderly lady who was well known and respected by her regular customers in the River Oaks community.

Most of my deliveries were to patients in hospitals, local funeral homes, and residential customers. It was a clean job with excellent hours, which was perfect for me to play with my dad's band on Friday and Saturday nights. I enjoyed the freedom of driving around Houston. On top of that, I loved seeing the smiles on people's faces when they would receive the beautiful arrangements Miss Polly created.

While working for Miss Polly, a strange incident occurred that would stay with me for years to come. One day, I had to explain why I didn't get a signature on the delivery receipt. As I described why I had purposely skipped out on the all-important signature, Miss Polly broke out laughing, which eased my tension.

So, why was she laughing at the incident? Well, I was delivering a casket spray to a local funeral home. I entered through a back door where the deliveries are typically dropped off, as I had done many times before. I tried to find someone to sign the receipt. However, I couldn't find anyone in the quiet funeral parlor. I approached a closed-door, knocked, and called out, "Hello, hello!" and got no response. So I opened the door to the room, and it was pitch black. It felt creepy in the room, so I reached against the side of the wall, to flip the light switch on. As the lights came on, my eyes bulged out and fixated on an elderly, naked dead man on a gurney. It scared the heck out of me. I rushed outside, jumped in the delivery truck, and high-tailed it back to the shop. At that point, I wasn't thinking about the signature.

As Miss Polly was listening and cracking up, she gave me these reassuring words of wisdom; "Albert, you should never be afraid of the dead because they can't hurt you. You should be afraid of the living; they are the ones that can hurt you." Later in life, I understood this.

In 1975, I left working for Miss Polly and began working at a well-known floral delivery service located on Richmond Ave. I became an experienced driver who knew most of the area's shortcuts, making it more accessible during rush hour. I knew the streets of Houston like the back of my hand, and I became good at my job.

At this new job, I worked alongside all kinds of diverse individuals from different backgrounds. Some were medical students in college with plans to one-day work in the medical center. Some were straight men and women, and some were gay. Regardless we learned how to respect each other's choices and opinions. Everyone seemed to get along well.

11

My First Born

In 1975 I made a decision to leave my dad's band. I wanted a taste of freedom and decided to venture out on my own. As he did with most things in life, he respected my choice. I had been performing with him for five years. It was time for me to spread my wings and fly.

My father and I built a deep bond as we performed together in some of the roughest cantinas in Northern California and Texas. The common bond we shared was music. I will always cherish those memories with him. I am forever grateful for the musical talent he taught me. Down the line, his grandchildren would also become musicians and play for the Lord. As I think of my father now, I wish I could go back and tell him how much I loved him. We just didn't do that, and it is something that I deeply regret.

After leaving my father's band, I was approached by other musicians, asking if I wanted to form a band. The proposition sounded pretty good to a young man learning his way about going off on his own, so I agreed. And right away, they wanted to head into a studio to record an album. I was both anxious and excited at the thought of it. It was not long before our four-person group had saved the five hundred dollars needed to record. After our vinyl album was fresh off the press, our songs were played on the local Spanish radio stations. It was an incredible feeling as we began to receive notoriety in some of the small towns.

It was an exciting time for me. We began touring across Texas and performed as opening acts for famous Tejano and Mexican Bands. At the time, it felt like that was what I was meant to do. Things seemed to be falling into place, and opportunities with women were falling into my lap. One-night stands became usual occurrences. Unbeknown to me, I had been watering the seeds of lust, sowed in me since my night in Boy's Town. It was developing into a full-blown addiction. I had a conceited mentality. I didn't know God by this point in my young adult life, nor was HE even a thought in my mind.

At the time, I was twenty years old and still living with my parents. They were working hard to keep a roof over our heads and food on the table. I had seen them struggle, and I was proud to be able to help our family. They had their hands full, looking after my younger siblings.

A year later, I met my first wife, Santos, through a groupie of the band. We were young; she was seventeen, and myself twenty-one. Immediately, the physical attraction was there. A couple months later, we got our own place and moved in together. We lived as husband and wife under the Texas rule of common-law marriage. There was no formal ceremony, but we held ourselves as a married couple, and all that entailed.

On March 17, 1978, my son, John Michael Garcia, was born. I was incredibly proud to be a father. I was happy that my son was born healthy, and I remember bragging at work and with the band. Santos also had a son, Carlos, from a previous marriage. He was a good kid; I loved him as my own son. Things were good. We were happy with our little family, living in a small duplex in the Montrose, but I had a dark side. I would work in the daytime with the delivery service and play nightclubs on the weekends, where temptation was plentiful, and my addiction was fed.

12

The Rumble

Now that I was living with my little family and providing for them, I hardly had time to see my father, as he wasn't at home when I had gone to visit my mom. One weekend, I felt a need to go out for a few hours. I decided to go see my dad's band perform. They were playing at a Mexican cantina in a rough area of Houston.

Upon entering the dance hall, I immediately recognized the sound of my father's style on his accordion. He and his band members were up on a small stage, which faced the dance floor. I knew the layout because we had performed there many times when I was a kid. Papi, our nickname for my dad, saw me and smiled. It was comforting to see how happy it made him that I stopped by to see him play. It had been three years since I was up there doing my thing next to him. With a rush of nostalgia, the memories came flooding back. Music was how I connected with my father growing up, and seeing him up there, I felt that connection as strong as ever.

I found a seat near a pool table where a couple of guys were deep into a game. My focus bounced back and forth between observing the game and watching my dad's band.

It wasn't long before my attention was elsewhere, as I eyed a group of guys entering the cantina. I instantly had a gut feeling they were looking for trouble. Sure enough, they began bothering the patrons.

Growing up, my dad always told us, "Trust your instincts," and at that moment, my instincts were telling me to keep a close eye on them. I never liked starting fights, which I had in common with my dad; however, I wasn't going to allow a few punks to intimidate me.

I sat there casually having a drink, waiting for my dad to take a break. I watched as the punks started to harass people. They were clearly trying to incite a fight. The bar began to clear out as they slowly made their way to different sections.

I, however, would not be relinquishing my seat nor my drink. To my right sat a friendly gentleman who had his beer resting on the same small table as mine. Suddenly, one of the troublemakers approached, violently slamming his beer can on our table, splashing beer all over my favorite shirt. I felt the heat of blood rushing to my head as anger pulsed through me. My friendly neighbor got the worst of it, with his hair completely soaked.

As I stood up to wipe the beer off my shirt, the punk got in my neighbor's face, beer still dripping down the side of his head. "Do you have a problem?" the jerk asked in Spanish. The guy simply remained calm and nodded. "*No, hay problema*," he answered. The punk then turned to face me, and before he opened his mouth, I punched him right in the face, which surprisingly stunned him.

Next thing you know, three of his *compadres* came

running to his aid. I spontaneously backed into the wall to avoid being surrounded. *The fight was on!* I began swinging and kicking like a wild cat just let out of a cage. It seemed as if I was fighting to the beat of my dad's Polka song.

The attackers were desperately trying hard to get me down on the floor. I knew that taking to the floor would be bad news for me, so I used every bit of strength to prevent it. Then the short one leaped over his *compadres* and latched on to my long hair, jerking me forward to the ground. Blows were coming from every direction as they began stomping on my head and body as well. I guess my dad and his band members hadn't seen what was going on.

I was in serious trouble. *Papi! Please! Look my way!* But I could still hear his music playing. Suddenly, the song stopped in the middle of the tune. *Yes! Finally!* Help was coming!

Finally, the beating stopped, and I was able to stand up. My dad was smashing a chair against the punks who had ganged up on me. All the while, his band members were giving some *street justice* to the thugs. They knew who I was, and the Golden Rule still stood. No one, absolutely no one, messed with the *musicos*. Other patrons began joining in as well, stomping on the bullies. The whole dance floor was chaotic, and it looked like a UFC rumble.

My dad's guitar player was engaged in a fistfight with one of my attackers. Enraged from the assault, I reached over, grabbed the punk's collar, and slugged him a couple of times in his face. We both went tumbling on top of a table from the force of the blows. Two elderly women, who had been seated at the table, scrambled for cover, screaming *"Aye Dios Mio!"* (Oh My God!)

The fighting finally settled down, and the defeated bullies bolted out of the cantina. It was not how I expected the night to go, but it did provide a bonding moment for my dad and me, which we continued to reminisce about over the years.

The best moment of the night, however, was when I arrived at my own front door. When I entered inside, and Santos saw my face all scratched up, my shirt ripped in half, and my hair out of whack, she frantically started shouting at me, "What the heck happened to you?" She was so emotionally distraught that she didn't even give me a chance to explain. I had never seen that side of her. She just kept repeating loudly, " What the heck happened to you?" I just couldn't stop laughing, seeing her like that. By the looks of it, it seemed that she was getting ready to give me another beat-down.

Even though there was humor to this story, I realized it could have turned out a lot worse for me. It wasn't uncommon for someone to pull a knife during a bar fight, as I had seen plenty of times while playing in my dad's band. I easily could have been stabbed. Now, I can say that I am so thankful to God for watching over me in that Mexican bar.

13

Brandi

Santos was a good wife to me. Yet, I was still out there womanizing and feeding my addiction. *What void was I trying to fill during those hazy nights?* God only knows as I was doing things a married man had no business doing. I began a short affair with a girl I met while playing at one of the Houston area clubs. She was younger than me, and I was not honest about being married. The conversation never came up. She didn't ask me, so I didn't bother to tell her. I did not want to admit that I was married, as that would force me to come to grips with the sin I was committing. Soon though, I would have no choice. I was naïve to think that nothing would come from the lifestyle I was living.

A couple of months later, I found out that the girl was pregnant. And in December, my second child, Brandi, was born. I kept my daughter's birth a secret from my wife. However, I couldn't keep that secret for long; Santos began to get suspicious. I had got myself into a mess, but when it came down to it, there was no way that I would deny my daughter.

Brandi was a gift to both her mother and me. From the mess I made came something beautiful. Although I messed up, Brandi was in no way a mistake. She was and still is a blessing. God had a plan for my daughter's life.

Psalms 139:16 (NIV) *Your eyes saw my unformed body; all the days ordained for me were written in your book before one of them came to be.*

Eventually, I told Santos everything. She was devastated, and rightfully so. She was angry and heartbroken, but she stuck around a little longer, hoping that I would change my ways. We would live together for 6 more years before she left me.

The Encounter

14

My mother-in-law passed away early on in our marriage. She was a devout Catholic. After her death, Santos kept her mother's rosary. I remember it being so precious to my mother-in-law. Later that cross would have a profound spiritual meaning in my life.

One day, I noticed the cross on the floor in our bedroom. At the time, I thought nothing of it. I picked it up and laid it on the dresser. A couple of days later, as I stopped in for lunch, I saw the cross on the floor again. I thought to myself, *this is strange*. So, I asked Santos why the cross was on the floor. She never gave me a logical explanation. It didn't make any sense. I knew it held sentimental value for her. I told her that she needed to put it in a safe place, so she insisted that I keep it. I bought a chain and put the cross on it.

Recollecting the cross now, it had black wood in its center, a shiny silver lining around the formation of the cross, and the image of Jesus engraved into it. I understood that it represented God. I couldn't quite grasp the feeling I got when I put it on. It didn't change me, but I began to think differently, perhaps, more spiritually.

I continued to wear the cross to work and while performing at nightclubs. I began to feel as if God was with me. I know now it was His Holy Spirit.

In 1983, after seven years of marriage, Santos chose to leave me and took the kids with her. She would later move with the boys to Wharton, Texas. Occasionally I would visit with Michael and Carlos. Two years later, we divorced. I was alone and hurt, but I was the only one to blame. I had betrayed her trust in me.

Several years later, she made it clear that she forgave me for all the hurt I caused her. I was, and still am, genuinely grateful for her forgiveness. I didn't deserve it, but she was gracious to give it anyway.

Broken-hearted, I was still living in Houston's Montrose district in a small efficiency apartment. I continued to wear the cross. It had personal, sentimental value to me, as it was a reminder of the love I had shared with Santos. More than that, it was symbolic of God's Spirit, which was still a new thing for me. I now believe God was preparing me for things to come.

While wearing the cross, an unusual spiritual presence continued to stir in me. Seemingly, it was affecting my way of thinking. I began to display overwhelming kindness for others. Women weren't part of my plan at that time. A peace came over me, which was surprising, considering Santos had recently left me, and it was still fresh on my mind. My outlook on life appeared different. I was finally contemplating moving in a healthy direction. I began to believe that maybe I was changed. Also, I remember telling friends that I was having an encounter with God.

One day, while on my usual deliveries for work, I was listening to the radio. A commercial caught my attention; the Houston Police Department was looking for a few good men or women to join the Police Academy. The requirement was a high school diploma, GED, or prior military or law enforcement experience. During this time, college credits were not a requirement. I would repeatedly hear this advertisement while I was working. I began to perceive that maybe God's presence was trying to express something to me. It felt like God was directing me to get my life right.

At the same time, God was making HIMSELF known in different ways each day: such as through a bumper sticker on the back of a car with the logo "In God We Trust." And certain songs would play on the radio, which became very inspirational to me; songs such as The Eye in The Sky and Every Breath You Take. The lyrics would resonate with me. I felt like God was actually watching me.

The commercial remained a constant thought embedded in my mind. I wondered if I actually had a chance to make it as a police officer. I had never been in trouble with the law; *surely, truancy wouldn't still be on my record, right?* Even still, I was an eighth-grade dropout. I did not even have a General Equivalency Diploma. I would need to pass the test to receive a GED to apply to the department.

I was feeling motivated to better myself. I was determined to give it a try. I remember praying, *if that's you, God, please help me to get my GED and be accepted into the police academy. At this point in my life, my prayers were superficial.*

I began to experience God's presence in my daily life. I began to think about Him and relate the world I knew to a world He created and controlled. Yet, I wasn't quite sure what was happening. Then, one day, I lost the cross. I had worn it for three months because it was precious to me. In my naïve understanding of the Holy Spirit, I actually believed that I lost God.

During this time, I received the news that the band's instruments were stolen in a burglary. My loss was a thousand dollar drum-set. In the '80s, a thousand dollars was a lot for me. I was sick about it. The police had no leads in the case, and it went unsolved. Since I had no money to purchase another drum-set, performing had come to an abrupt halt. I often wondered if this was God's way of getting me to quit the band and move my life in the direction He had planned for me.

I started praying more and reading a pocket-sized Bible I had received somewhere along the way. A specific verse that got my attention was *Matthew 7:7 (NIV)*, *"Ask, and it will be given to you; seek, and you will find; knock, and the door will be opened to you."* Reading this scripture gave me a sense of encouragement to continue to better myself. I memorized the scripture because it really touched my spirit.

A few months later, I was delighted to find out that I had passed the test to obtain my GED. I had prayed earnestly for this, and God answered my prayer. I was thrilled to finally get it, but even more so to know that God heard me. This caused my faith in God to increase. I didn't feel so lonely knowing that He was with me.

My encounter with God was new to me. I was hungry to learn more about Him. I went into a bookstore to buy books on spirituality. Sadly, the books I bought were not so much about God but about The Spiritual realm. Those books had a negative influence on my mind. I was trying to do good, but the enemy had other plans.

15

The Tempter

On a winter day in 1983, I ran into an old acquaintance named Francisco. It had been eight years since I had last seen him in my old stomping grounds. Back in the day, I remember he always dressed sharp, and he was much older than my friends and me. He lived a rough life of drinking and drugs. He had walked dark paths, ultimately resulting in him doing hard time. As we chatted about old times, he told me he just got out of prison. It was a fresh start for him, yet here he was right back to his old ways. I saw darkness in his eyes; something didn't feel quite right. Not knowing what the feeling was, I ignored it. He invited me to go with him to some strip clubs where several female dancers worked for him. I was trying to join the Police Academy. I was getting prepared to apply, but I still agreed to hook up with him later; after all, he was an old friend.

That night, I picked him up in my car, and we drove to the Galleria area, just west of Downtown Houston. While we were in the parking lot in front of the club, he pulled out a pill and said, "Take this." Immediately I felt uneasiness in my spirit. I told him I didn't do drugs. He said, "Take half the pill, and it will make you feel good inside the club." I repeated, "No, man, I don't do drugs. I will get a drink inside the place!" Finally, he relented, and we got out of the car to make our way into the club.

Entering inside, I felt something wrestling within myself. I knew God had been trying to speak to me recently, but here I was still tangled in the ever-tightening grip of sin and lust. *Wasn't I trying to change my life?* The Devil was tugging at my flesh. He was trying to get me to choose the path of sin because he knew I was on the verge of changing my life. He knew just what bait to dangle before me, *women*.

Francisco did not know that I wanted to join the police department, and honestly, I didn't want him to know. I was there for only one thing. I wanted to meet a chick. I followed his lead, and we sat at a table near the stage. I was never one to go to strip clubs to find girls; in that regard, it was usually smooth sailing as a musician. I didn't have to look for girls. Most women came to me.

Unexpectedly, my mind shifted to Santos and the kids. They were gone now. I had also recently quit the band. *This lifestyle is not my way anymore*, I thought. It was like I awoke from a daze of deception. I remember seeing the girl dancing on the stage and thinking, *what the heck am I doing here?* Francisco leaned in close with a sinister smirk on his face. "That's one of my girls," he told me. He stared at me and motioned with his hand toward the beautiful woman saying, "You can have all this." Next, he pulled a wad of money out from his coat pocket and continued his attempt to entice me. "You know how you keep these girls loyal to you? You make them feel good by giving them cocaine, and they'll do anything for it," he said. I glanced into his eyes as he offered me this lifestyle and saw that they were glowing red. An eerie feeling came over me as if time stood still. Now, you probably think I must have taken Francisco's pill after all. God is my witness. I didn't! God was trying to reach me; He was trying to awaken me from the daze of temptation that I had lived under for so many years. But I didn't realize that just yet.

A short time later, we were at a different strip joint. So, why did I wind up at another club with the *tempter* trying to lure me back into my old sin? Easy, the deceiver knew how to use my weaknesses against me. He knew it would be difficult for me to resist the lust-driven desire of a woman's company. I was lonely and craved the pleasure of a one-night stand.

While inside the club, I met a young Cuban girl with seductive long black hair. She was drinking alone at the bar while Francisco was backstage visiting "his girls," as he called them. I started up an innocent conversation with my new friend. She said she was here visiting from Cuba. She spoke Spanish, and so did I. We chatted a bit about random things, and then she asked if I knew of a place to go dancing. She was forward, and I liked that. The deceiver once again was dangling that bait; he knew I'd bite every time. Hooked, we mutually decided to take our new friendship elsewhere. I told Francisco I was leaving, and that was the last time I ever saw him.

My new lady friend and I left in my car and ended up on lower Westheimer Boulevard. We were unable to find a place that was open for dancing. We did, however, find a gay club that was still open. It wasn't my typical scene, but I wasn't ready for the night to end. We headed inside to have a drink. Things got uncomfortable for us soon after we arrived. Men who were dressed in drag were shouting obscenities at my friend. They seemed to be bothered by our presence there, and we both recognized that we were not welcome. We stuck out like a sore thumb.

By the time I realized that we needed to head out before trouble struck, my female companion was tipsy. I advised her it would be best for us to leave, but she wanted to finish her drink. The bartender then caught me off guard by asking if we were cops. Maybe he thought we were undercover. I told him no! I thought to myself, *I want to be a cop.* The bartender then suggested we leave. The crowd was getting loud, and it was clear we were unwelcome. Because she was tipsy, she began arguing back with them, and things were getting out of hand. *This woman is trouble,* I thought anxiously, trying to get her to leave. During the commotion, she unknowingly dropped her passport a couple of times. For safekeeping, I placed it in my pants pocket, not thinking much of it.

As we were trying to leave, the men dressed in drag grew increasingly aggressive towards us. I was doing my best to exit quickly and escort the woman outside safely. But the men followed us, shouting and cursing. She was exchanging profanities with them as well. Once outside, standing by the road, the situation escalated quickly; I knew we needed to leave right away. I told her, "Come on! Let's go now! I have your passport." I fished it out of my pocket and showed it to her, trying to convince her to leave, and I guess she thought I stole it. She was drunk by that point, and she freaked out, snatched the passport out of my hands, and began physically assaulting me. As this was happening, an HPD cruiser drives by and sees the disturbance. I remember watching the police unit make an abrupt U-turn and turn on their siren. By this time, I was thinking, *OH MY GOD, what have I gotten into? My heart began to pound. I was about to jeopardize my dream of becoming a police officer because of the situation I found myself in.*

It's funny, isn't it? But I wasn't laughing. I believed in God, but even non-believers who get themselves into trouble sometimes call on God. And that's precisely what I did. I was scared to go to jail. Two police officers approached us, and they ordered me to put my hands on the hood. I complied immediately. Internally, I was pleading with God to save me from this situation. I knew it was my fault because of my poor choices, but still, I was looking for Him to get me out of this mess.

I looked over at my female companion, and she was acting belligerent with one of the officers. I was feeling disappointed in myself at this point. *How did I end up in this mess? Why can't I resist the temptation of lust?* At one point, I saw her spit at one of the officers. She was immediately placed in handcuffs and put in the back seat of the patrol car. The officer interacting with me asked, "What the hell is going on?" I proceeded to explain in earnest what had happened that evening, how we had met, and why we ended up at a gay club. I described what transpired once we arrived, and how she lost it when she thought I had taken her passport and began hitting me. I sincerely expressed with my voice that I did not want any trouble with the law because I was trying to get into the Houston Police Academy.

The officer saw I was not intoxicated and was being truthful, so I was told to leave. *You bet*, I thought, and I rushed my butt right out of there. As I walked away, I glanced to see the girl and saw she was crying. The officers had arrested her. I was just relieved for it to be over. I never saw her again.

On the drive home, I was thanking God. I knew I had made bad choices, and the night could have ended very differently. I truly believed God had saved me from going to jail that night. I drove in silence, just lost in my thoughts. I reflected on how strangely the day had unfolded. I knew better, but when the opportunity presented itself, I couldn't resist. A heaviness settled on me as I drove. I felt as if the tempter knew I was trying to better myself and desperately wanted me to choose *la Vida Loca*. I wondered if God was teaching me a lesson that night. One thing was for sure, God showed up for me. I knew He was the reason I was free and not in handcuffs.

Many years later, I had heard that someone killed Francisco in prison. It was tough for me to understand because I knew he died in his wicked ways; he died, not knowing there was another way. It burdened my heart deeply. It could have easily been how my story ended. I thank God that He had another plan for me.

1Corinthians 10:11 So, if you think you are standing firm, be careful that you don't fall!

As you can see, if I had gone to jail that night, I would have forfeited any chance of getting accepted into the Police Academy. Thank you, Lord, for rescuing me, even in my sinful nature. God is good, and He is faithful. He knew I had work to do for His glory.

16

The Academy

In the spring of 1984, I applied to the Houston Police Department Recruiting Division. The initial process was a sit-down interview with a recruiter. The recruiter checked each applicant's height and weight to ensure those measurements were proportionate to the standards. I assume they felt certain body types were less suited for the job. As such, some applicants were rejected on the spot, and some were disqualified for other reasons.

If you made it past the initial phase, then the lengthy, detailed application process began. I would have to undergo a reading comprehension test, a physical agility test, submit to a polygraph examination, a psychological exam, and a health examination with a city doctor. The recruiter, who was also a police officer, then checked each applicant's credit history and conducted an in-depth background investigation.

After completing all of the tasks, there was nothing left to do but wait to hear back from the recruiter, who was hopefully calling to congratulate you on your acceptance into the training academy.

About two months later, while at work, my recruiter contacted me with the good news. I had passed the application process and was officially accepted to begin training. He instructed me to report to the academy on July 9, 1984, with cadet class #122.

I was calm and collected on the phone, responding, "Yes, sir." But as soon as I hung up, the excitement settled in. *"I'm in," I exclaimed to my coworkers!* I felt so accomplished.

This was big! It was a fresh start, a new path. Also, I would soon be making a lot more money. *Thank you, God!*

God was on my mind for sure. I was so grateful for what was happening in my life. It was evident that He was doing something. I knew He was listening. He had answered my prayers. Soon, though, the challenging work would begin. Getting in was only the first step in the grueling process. Training would push me to new challenges. I had no idea how educationally challenging it would be. I was prepared to face physically demanding situations. However, I was unaware of the importance of having a sound academic mind.

At the training academy, recruits had to complete six months of physical endurance training and were also required to pass the academic courses. Every Monday morning, the cadets were tested on material from the previous week's lectures. All trainees were required to achieve a passing grade, and if a cadet failed three exams, it was grounds for discharge or resignation. My stress level was at an all-time high surrounding these exams. During classroom hours, I began to fall behind in note-taking. I couldn't keep up with the pace of the lectures. Spelling was an issue for me, which made note-taking a longer process. The classroom part was not my strength, but my physical agility was exceptional. Although I excelled in every physical challenge, every aspect is essential during police training.

It wasn't long before I had failed two exams. I began to worry that *I might not make it.*

As another Monday came; it was do or die time for the exam. My palms felt sweaty, and my mind was racing. *Focus, Garcia!* I gave it everything I had, but my stomach was in knots after finishing the test. *I think it's over. I think I failed.*

The results were typically given out after lunch. We were all hanging out in the gym, patiently waiting to know who was still in or out. Then, one of the training instructors walked in with a straight facial expression. There was not much chatter as we anxiously awaited our fate. The room froze as the instructor yelled in a loud authoritative voice, "Garcia! Dress up and report to the Sergeant's office." I felt my heart sink. Everyone went silent. *Were any other names going to be called?* No. Mine was the only one. I knew what it meant, but I hoped against fate that I would be joining my classmates the following day.

Approaching the Sergeant's office, I followed procedure and announced my presence, "Cadet Garcia!" to gain approval before entering his office. Access was granted, and nervously, I entered. Reading his face, I immediately knew it was terrible news. I was instructed to have a seat next to his desk. My heart pounded hard in my chest. I tried to prepare myself for what my gut knew was coming.

The Sergeant said, in a sad voice, "Garcia, you did not make it. I'm sorry to say you've failed three exams already." For a moment, I sat there silently, both stunned and sad. *I hadn't cut it.* I was feeling low and sorry for myself. But then I heard Sergeant say, "But you can come back in one year and try again!"

I was then asked to sign a form and collect all my belongings from the classroom and my locker. I walked, as if almost in slow motion, deep in thought. I knew I was struggling academically, but still, I had desperately clung to hope for a miracle; however, it hadn't come that day.

I was in a daze. Everyone else was still gathered in the gym, and I was glad for that. I was too embarrassed to face anyone. Soon my classmates would hear what they already knew; I had failed.

The large parking lot was quiet and empty as I slowly made my way to my car, feeling defeated. Sadly, this was not the first time I had failed at something. I thought to myself, *maybe it wasn't meant to be!*

I thought back to my days of skipping school. I had

no idea, at the time, the repercussions it would have. It had come back to bite me.

As I entered the quietness of my car, I cried like a baby. In that very instant, I had come to realize how passionately I wanted to be a Houston Police Officer. But at the time, it felt like my dream was shattered. I had come up short. I was spiraling into a tornado of self-pity crying, there in my car. Then, like a soft inner whisper, I heard the voice of God say, *"Remember, you can come back again."* Suddenly, God's presence filled my car and silenced my doubt. A sense of peace and purpose came over me. Driving home, those words played over in my mind and lit a fire in my soul. I prayed to God that I would be back!

17

Frances

A month after failing the Police Academy, I was at my cousin's house in the Heights area, still feeling sorry for myself. We were outside talking as a little red car drove up to the front of the house. The driver was a nice-looking young woman with a very intriguing smile. I wasn't sure what to make of her.

She had come to pick my aunt up for church. As my aunt introduced us, I learned her name was Frances. She smiled and politely invited my cousin and me to attend church with them. My cousin and I looked at each other with hesitation and declined the offer. Little did I know, God would later use Frances as a vessel to get me closer to Him.

Though I wasn't attending church, I was feeling God's presence in my life. I continued to stay away from the nightclubs and had gone back to my old job with the delivery service. I'll admit it was embarrassing having to return and face my former co-workers. I felt like a loser, ashamed I had failed the academy because of my lack of education. I carried the deep humiliation of coming up short of my dream to become a cop. But that didn't extinguish my passion. I was still determined to return to the academy one day with God's help. I had witnessed evidence of the power of God when I was in the academy the first time. I knew God had been with me then, and I was confident He would help me to return. There was no doubt in my mind; becoming a police officer was my calling!

While hanging out with my cousin one day, he told me Frances had continued to invite us to church. I felt an urge in my gut telling me we should accept her invitation. I know now that it was a tug in my spirit, a push from God in the right direction. I told my cousin, "Come on, let's go. What do we have to lose?"

We jumped in my 1972 Mercury Cougar and headed to Frances' church, the Life Tabernacle Pentecostal. After several Sundays of attending with her, a young pastor approached me and asked if I wanted to get baptized. He also asked if I wanted to accept Jesus as my Savior. I was familiar with God. I knew in my heart that He was real. But I didn't have much knowledge of who this Jesus was. I was interested in learning more about Him. I knew baptism was an essential step closer to God, so I agreed with the pastor to get baptized.

On the day I was baptized, Frances was there with me. She was so proud that I had accepted Jesus as my Lord and Savior. When I asked Jesus to be my Savior, I spoke those words with my mouth, but I don't believe my heart knew exactly what that meant. As a result of that declaration of faith, I had new expectations of abstaining from sex and lustful temptations. I had already been trying my best to do that, but now I had made a promise to God.

I wasn't sure how one was supposed to feel when they got saved. I did not feel any different. Admittedly, I had expected some big, defining moment to happen, like a bright light shining down on me, or something out of the ordinary. Obviously, I was still new in my faith!

As time went on, Frances and I became good friends. Our friendship slowly changed into something more profound, and we began to admit to ourselves our attraction for each other. She was soft-spoken, with a kind spirit, and was never afraid to tell people about Jesus.

Our relationship continued as a friendly flirtation until she invited me to her co-worker's wedding one day. You can call it our first date. The conversations with her came easy. We enjoyed each other's company, and we both shared our stories. She told me she was divorced and had two daughters, Jessica and Jennifer. I remember being nervous to tell her about my time as a musician and the terrible choices I had made in those late nights at the clubs. She had a way of making me feel at ease, though. I confessed my past and explained I had also been married before. I told her about my daughter, Brandi, and my son, Michael. I shared my dream of becoming a police officer and how I had recently flunked out of the academy. I expected her to lose interest in me after my revelations and quickly walk in the opposite direction, but that wasn't the kind of person she was. Frances was smart, educated, and kind. She wasn't fazed at all. Instead, she responded by offering to help me achieve my dream. I was blown away. At that moment, I began to trust that God had put her in my life for a purpose.

In 1985, we were married, and one year later, our son, Albert, was born.

Frances and I both continued to pray. We clung to the promise that I would become a Houston police officer one day in God's will. I was grateful for her continued support. Confidently, I believed our prayers would one day come to fulfillment.

Frances was an outstanding mother to my son, Albert,

and my step-daughter's Jessica and Jennifer. She was a loyal, loving wife, and I knew I was blessed. We were happy. Life was good.

18

Cadet Class 137

I decided it was time to better my education and started attending college courses in Criminal Justice. I actually sold my 1972 Cougar to pay for tuition. I registered at Houston Community College, where I excelled in my studies. Two years later, I applied for the Peace Officer's program at the University of Houston. While I attended U of H full-time, Frances made sure our finances were paid, and our kids were cared for. She then spent her nights helping me with my studies. I was happy with my new family and busy with my homework; there was no time to think about the kind of life I had lived before. We continued to go to church, and our family was doing quite well.

As soon as I received my Peace Officer's certification from U of H, I was hired on with the Houston Independent School District as a Substance Abuse Monitor assigned to Lamar High School. It wasn't my dream, but it was a step in the right direction. At the time, the HPD Training Academy was experiencing a hiring freeze, so I would have to wait to reapply. Though, my ambitions hadn't changed; I would return and attempt to pass the academy a second time.

Sadly, four years into our marriage, impure thoughts slowly began creeping back into my mind. Not long after, I engaged in a fling and was able to keep it a secret from Frances. I even attempted to erase it from my mind. Even though I was successful in my deceit, God knew exactly what I had done!

Luke 8:17 (NIV) *For there is nothing hidden that will not be disclosed and nothing concealed that will not be known or brought out into the open.*

In 1989, after being closed to applicants for three and a half years, the Houston Police Academy finally reopened; however, the qualifications had changed. Each applicant was required to have at least 60 hours of college. Whew! Only a month earlier, I had completed my 62 college hours. Thank God!

I applied to the academy for the second time at the age of thirty-three. I passed the entry round and later received notice from the recruiter to report to the academy on October 18, 1989. I was to begin my training with HPD Cadet Class #137. I was back again! This time, though, I would have the confidence of proper education and would have no trouble passing.

On April 18, 1990, my long-awaited dream came true, and I graduated with my class, and was officially an officer of the Houston Police Department. I knew with absolute certainty that it was with God and Frances' help that I succeeded. It was a great time as we celebrated God's faithfulness in answering our prayers. I knew that God was real without question, and I was filled with a new sense of direction and a desire to please Him.

Unfortunately, my spiritual roots were shallow. I hadn't dealt with the critical issues or taken the time to truly commit my heart to the Lord. I spoke it with my words, but here again, not with my heart. I went to church, and I prayed, but those were just religious actions. I did want to be an honorable man. What I was missing, though, was the intimate relationship with Jesus. I hadn't spent time studying God's word. I did not have the Holy Spirit's guidance or even know what that meant. If only I would have kept my head forward and my eyes fixed on Jesus. Life gets messy when you allow your attention to drift to worldly things.

I was a good police officer, determined and focused. I wish that I could have said the same for my title as a husband.

19

The Rock

After being officially sworn in as a police officer, it was time to report to my assigned station for a six-month probation period and the field-training program. I was assigned to the Northeast substation, which had been my first choice.

The Northeast part of Houston was notoriously one of the roughest areas due to high gang activity. My brothers-in-blue informed me that the substation had the nickname The Rock. I later asked a senior officer about the name's significance and was told the station was known for being union strong.

The beginning stages of field training consisted of riding with training officers (FTO's) out on patrol, for a twelve-week phase.

Once we completed the required hours of patrolling with our assigned FTO, the senior officers then tested our knowledge in the training evaluation phase. The evaluation measured the rookie's quality of performance, the safety measures taken, and if correct procedures were followed. The emphasis-training program was highly critical regarding each officer's safety when patrolling the streets. The saying was, "We want to make sure we go home safe."

Like any other rookie, I couldn't wait to get off probation. I was ready to get out there on my own and do some crime-fighting.

Fresh out of the probation period, I was assigned a regular shift from 1500 to 2300 hours (3pm-11pm), with Tuesdays and Wednesdays off. These weren't the best days, but it didn't matter; I was excited to fulfill the vision God had placed on my life.

I strutted into the station on my first official day, pumped and itching to get out there. *I thought, today, I finally ride alone.* Calm and collected on the outside, I listened as the shift Sergeant made roll call and read aloud a few bulletins (crime alerts) to be on the lookout for. I then walked over to the radio room, where an officer handed me my police radio and keys to my regular assigned patrol car. The next process was to advise the dispatcher, via radio, that I was signing on duty, "One-man unit 9C33e on duty."

Time to get after it! First, I did a quick inspection of my patrol car's equipment and carried out other standard procedures. I was loaded with my ticket books, a clipboard, flashlight, forms, and other necessary gear. I cranked up the patrol car and drove off to District 9, the area near the Port of Houston. I remember pulling up to the first traffic light, just blocks from the station, and taking a moment to reflect, thinking to myself, *well, this is it!*

Just seconds later, a citizen was already flagging me down. From my observation, it appeared to be a disturbance outside a small grocery store at the corner of Kelly and Hirsh road.

I quickly radioed the dispatcher to hold me out On-View Disturbance and provided the location. The disturbance was immediately settled at the scene. It was a minor customer dispute over being short-changed by the clerk. I then advised the dispatcher that I was back en-route to my beat.

That call was a judgment call. No crime was committed. A senior officer once told me, "Common sense is necessary to be a cop." Experience later taught me just how true that was.

I enjoyed working alone. However, one day at The Rock, I bumped into Officer Johnny, an old cadet classmate I met in 1984. Johnny was from Class #122 when I failed the academy the first time. I was just getting started while he already had a little over five years under his patrol belt.

Johnny seemed surprised to see that I had returned, seeing that I was booted from the academy the last time we crossed paths. We got along well, and a year later, we became patrol partners, which was called a two-man unit. I learned quite a few things from his crime-fighting abilities that would help shape me as a cop.

Looking back at my law enforcement career, God always had my back and continued to show favor through officers He placed in my path. I was able to learn valuable insights from their God-given talents.

Johnny was a dedicated crime-fighter and a skillful street cop who was good at solving cases. He worked investigations like a seasoned detective, even though his assigned duties were patrolling the beat. One of Johnny's many knacks was solving robberies, which later became an interest of mine.

Case in point, one cold evening on solo patrol, I

received a call from the dispatcher regarding an aggravated robbery at a Mexican bakery. I arrived at the scene where the suspect was gone on arrival (GOA).

I interviewed the female victim working the register and gathered the preliminary report's information. From interviewing the complainant, I learned the suspect's Method of Operation (M.O.) was that he lingered inside the business while pretending to be waiting for his ride.

The suspect's intention was to wait for the customers to leave and then approach the cashier alone. The suspect displayed a pistol and pointed it at the clerk's face while demanding all the register's money. The clerk, fearful for her life, immediately complied with the suspect's demands.

As I asked questions regarding the suspect's description, the clerk trembled persistently. It always bothered me to see a victim of a crime like that! Despite being shaken up, she clearly distinctively remembered a tattoo on the robber's right ear lobe. After I finished gathering the information for my police report, I gave her a case number.

A week later, having filled Johnny in on the bakery robbery details, we heard a dayshift officer had recently completed a robbery report for a grocery store. It so happens it was just five blocks away from the bakery robbery. It appeared the suspect had struck again.

We reviewed the grocery store robbery report at the station, and we discovered that a male suspect robbed the cashier after loitering inside the store. And guess what? The suspect had a tattoo on his right ear lobe.

With certainty, Johnny declared we had a serial robber on our hands. And as usual, he was right.

A few days later, while Johnny and I were patrolling the beat, we received a call from the police dispatcher to a disturbance regarding a child custody issue. The location was in the same vicinity where the two robberies had occurred.

When we arrived on the scene, we observed a male

standing outside the home. The man claimed to be the person who called the police, and he explained the nature of his disturbance, which was a child custody battle with his former wife.

While conducting our interview, a particular feature of the male who placed the call to the dispatcher caught our attention. As I made eye contact with Johnny, I knew we were on the same page. We finished our questioning and walked back to the police car. "Partner, do you see what I see?" Johnny inquired. I nodded. The male had a tattoo on his right ear lobe, and he fit the description given from the two robberies. We knew we could possibly be looking at our suspect.

At that point, Johnny told me, "Partner, I believe they need a police report," as he gave a side wink that said plenty. He walked back and requested the man's identification for the report. We then provided the male with a case number and left the scene.

Excitedly, we raced back to the station, discussing the possibility of having a lead on both robberies. Once at the station, we ran a criminal background on the listed male and *bingo*! The man in question had a criminal history, and what do you know? He previously did time for robbery.

Here was where Johnny set in motion my Course 101 in detective work. He contacted the Robbery Division, informed the shift detective of a possible lead in both robberies, and asked if we could work the cases. Right away, they said yes. I later learned that most detectives are overwhelmed with caseloads and welcomed all the help or potential leads that they could get.

After receiving the detective's approval to work the robberies, Johnny obtained a profile mug shot from our potential suspect's previous arrest. He then demonstrated how to construct a picture lineup to show both of the victims. There were six photos in the array; Johnny explained the other five individuals in the photo array must have similar characteristics to the main suspect.

Johnny asked me, "Partner, where do you want to position our male suspect's photo on the lineup?" I randomly picked where to put the suspect's photo. But later in my career, I typically had a favorite number for the photo spread placement.

The next phase was showing the photo lineup to the victims for possible identification. It was always important to explain to the victims that they were not obligated to identify a culprit. They were only to point to the picture if they recognized the offender on the lineup.

Through the years, while showing photo spreads, I always remember hoping with anticipation to get a positive identification of a suspect. More times than not, my intuition was usually right on point.

In this case, both victims from the robberies positively identified the suspect who robbed them. As Johnny explained, the next step was to file charges to obtain an arrest warrant from The District Attorney's Office. While at the prosecutor's intake office, we describe the probable cause and elements of the crime. Once the prosecutor accepted the charges for two counts of aggravated robbery, we walked the affidavit over to a judge for a signature.

Having completed the time-consuming process of obtaining the arrest warrants with a copy of the court order in hand, we were ready to rock and roll and arrest the suspect. Johnny and I had a good address; we located the male and arrested him without any resistance. Afterward, a thrilling feeling of accomplishment rushed through me.

Several months later came the subpoena to go to trial. It was time to testify against the defendant. Being a rookie, Johnny allowed me to get experience, so I was chosen to testify.

First, the jury panel heard the victims' accounts of

the frightening ordeal of the armed robberies. Then came my turn to take the stand and give testimony. At first, I was a little tense, but as time drew on, it became easy.

I was proud to be a Houston police officer. I learned that eye contact with the jurors was vital when explaining the facts, thereby demonstrating your testimony's credibility.

In this case, the jury returned a guilty verdict and sentenced the defendant to 20 years in prison. Justice was complete. A dangerous person was removed from the streets.

After walking out of the courthouse building and back inside our patrol car, Johnny and I gave each other high-fives in celebration of what we believed was a job well done.

A few weeks later, Johnny and I received a commendation letter from the trial prosecutor for our efforts in solving both cases.

Sincerely, I can say that solving those robberies with Johnny played a vital role in my career as a cop. Thanks, partner.

Johnny and I were partners on patrol for almost three years before he officially transferred to investigations. Little did we know, years later, he would return to patrol, where we would work together solving several high-profile cases in the Kingwood area.

Working the Beat

As a rookie officer, I quickly discovered that it wasn't wise to respond to a situation led by emotions, especially when handling hostile confrontations. Believe me, some individuals will test one's patience while working in law enforcement. In those instances, it is smart to stay calm and fully take in the situation before reacting.

While working street patrol, I dealt with people from all walks of life. In the more impoverished neighborhoods, I became familiar with the residents who were the keepers of peace and those who weren't. Most of the locals in those communities supported the cops and rallied behind police efforts to reduce crime, predominantly drug-related offenses. Crack-cocaine, meth, and heroin had gotten so bad in some areas that many parents feared their children would get involved in dealing or using drugs. Sadly, very few were willing to talk with an officer for fear of the drug lord's retribution.

Unfortunately, drugs were a common way of life in low-income communities. Whether from lack of means to afford a different lifestyle, doubt for a better future, or fear of the gangs and drug lords, some teenagers choose a dark path of crime and drugs.

Police stations were overrun with reports of drug-related offenses. In one of the communities I patrolled, we received constant calls from a concerned father, notifying us of a street-level drug dealer selling at the local corner store. He was determined to keep his son off that dark path.

It was a frustrating cycle. We would arrest one dealer, tag the dope, and process him only to return to the corner store three hours later to see a new dealer selling. In some of those districts, it was an endless battle.

Police officers feel the burden of those situations. I sympathized with the parents who spent their days and nights hoping and praying their child wouldn't get wrapped up in the drug life or killed by someone from a rival gang. As we spoke with the mothers and fathers, the desperation was evident in their voices. I understood their frustrations.

As challenging as it was working in the more dangerous parts of town, I learned many valuable lessons. I quickly learned the importance of focusing and not letting my emotions interfere with my job. If I lost focus for even a split second, it could have cost me my life. In situations like those, scenes often became very intense and overwhelming, which sometimes weighed heavily on officers.

On one Saturday, as I was riding solo due to a shortage of manpower, a fellow officer received a domestic violence assault call; a male had assaulted his mother. Since he was also a one-man unit, I notified the dispatcher that I would be checking by with the officer.

Upon interviewing the 40-year-old, crying mother, we observed welt marks on her face, presumably from the assault. As she emotionally explained the attack, she indicated her adult son didn't work and spent most of his time drinking. She directed us to a bedroom where he was sleeping.

As we entered the room to make an arrest, we advised the male to wake up and get out of the bed. Immediately, he refused. My partner grabbed his left arm and tried to lift him up while I secured his right arm. Then, abruptly, he shoved my partner and attempted to flee. He continued to resist arrest aggressively. In a stern voice, I uttered an expletive choice of words along with saying, "Beating on your mother punk, go ahead and beat on us!" After wrestling with him for a moment, he was successfully subdued and handcuffed without further incident.

After taking him into custody, I wondered if I had allowed my personal feelings to get the best of me. It's not always easy to remain detached from certain situations, especially after seeing a tearful mother's bruised face. I thought to myself, *how could someone rough up his or her mother?*

21

The Chase

I was falling into a routine as I worked my usual 3 to 11pm shift. One cold rainy day, with a little over two years with the department, I had just pulled up to my district, and I thought to myself, this is a good day for some warm donuts and a hot cup of coffee. I know you're thinking; that fits right into the stereotype of cops loving donuts. Some of us enjoyed a glazed one to kick-start our shift. Add a hot cup of coffee, and I was raring to go!

Enough donut talk, let's get to the real story.

It was almost a daily occurrence for patrol officers to respond to stolen vehicle reports in those days. General Motors were typically the vehicles that the thieves' would target. Their usual MO was to bust the steering column and crank up the ignition with a screwdriver.

I had just pulled out of the donut shop's drive-through and entered the I-10 service road when I observed a blue Buick driving with the windows rolled down. That wouldn't typically be alarming, except it was raining *cats and dogs!* So, I decided to cruise beside the Buick. The male driver was alone in the car. His eyes bulged out at me as we made eye contact, thus furthering my suspicion that possibly the vehicle was stolen. As someone once said, the eyes are the windows of the soul and they show intent.

Upon further observation, I noticed the steering column covered with a towel. I slowly backed off to get behind the vehicle and radioed the police dispatcher to check a plate for a possible *rolling stolen*. Within seconds, the dispatcher responded, "Be advised, this car was just reported stolen from a church parking lot." "That's clear," I replied. "Get a unit to check by with me. We are traveling westbound on the service road!"

Immediately, my back-up unit was right behind me.

The driver of the stolen vehicle repeatedly looked in his rearview mirror. He was anxious. My adrenaline rushed as I considered the possibility of a chase. Lo and behold, as I lit up my emergency lights, the pursuit began! Sirens were blaring, and my blood was pumping as I announced over the police radio, "Be advised, the driver is refusing to stop!"

The pursuit quickly turned dangerous. The driver was blazing 55 mph through busy intersections, running red lights. I had to look at the bigger picture. Innocent lives were in danger, and the weather condition wasn't helping. I started to consider disengaging from the chase. With innocent motorists at risk of severe injury or death, was it worth it? I didn't believe so.

I notified the dispatcher, "Be advised, I am terminating the pursuit." At that very moment, the driver lost control, skidded off the road, and crashed into the front entrance of an abandoned church. It was ironic, indeed.

I radioed the dispatcher "Be advised, the suspect cracked up!" My back-up unit and I arrested the uninjured perpetrator.

Years later, I caught myself thinking about this incident. It was unusual that the suspect stole the car from one church and then crashed into another church. Could this have been divine intervention? I believe that it was. Thank God no one was hurt.

22

The House Fire

By now, I had a few years on the force and had responded to various calls, such as homicides, suicides, and accidental fatalities. As a cop, you never know quite what to expect when arriving at a scene. We saw it all too; bizarre, humorous, sad, gruesome, you name it. It just depended on the type of call you received. It became normal not to show emotions after seeing something awful.

You could say we became desensitized to challenging scenes. Our job was to assure that those involved in the incident would stay calm. We were trained not to emotionally put ourselves into the situation; however, one specific call made accomplishing that hard. Seeing a dead child deeply affects even the most hardened cops. It's the call no one wants to get. Still, to this day, images from this scene remain burned into my memory.

It was a cold winter night. While patrolling my beat, I observed a house on fire in a neighborhood. As I drove closer to the scene, I could see several fire trucks with their emergency lights on and water hoses lying across the roadway. I switched my emergency lights on and positioned my vehicle to block street access from oncoming traffic. I radioed into the dispatcher to hold me out at the scene and began making my way towards the house. As I walked closer, I could see the fire was still actively burning, and the firemen were dousing the flames.

Crowds were gathered along the sidewalks watching the fire intensely. The flames were quickly engulfing the entire home, which was a one-story brick structure.

On the front of the property laid an older man on the damp cold ground. The paramedics were placing an oxygen mask on his face, and I could hear the man murmur, *"Get my kids!"* Simultaneously, a lady approached me and advised me that he was a pastor.

Once the fire was out, we had to wait for the firefighters to declare it safe to enter. I then walked towards the rear of the house. The firemen were still searching for a ten-year-old boy. I knew at this point that we were most likely recovering a body rather than rescuing a child. Carefully, I entered the house through the back door, figuring I would assist with my flashlight.

It was dark inside the house, and the heat from the fire was still evident. As I shined my flashlight around the structure, I could see certain areas still smoldering. I then heard a fireman say in a sad, far-off voice, *"I found Him"*. He made his way past me, with his head hung low, and his facial expression was somber. I knew it was not good news. *"Where is he?"* I asked softly. The firefighter pointed in the direction of another room in the back section of the house; I guess I wasn't emotionally prepared for what I was about to face.

I was alone upon entering the quiet, dark room. I moved carefully, watching my every step while trying to adjust my vision in the darkness. As I got close, a strong smell of burnt human flesh filled my nostrils. I recoiled at that stench that I had smelled at a previous crime scene. I paused for a moment to maintain my composure. My eyes fixed on the ruins of a small-coiled bed. The visibility was very dim, and I was having trouble finding the body.

I directed my light towards the opposite side of the bed frame. I knew what I would find, but it was shocking to see the charred remains of a small body. I was horrified as my eyes took in the child's remains. It was a figure kneeling next to his little bed in a praying position. His knees were on the floor, his arms bent, and his hands clasped together. He had been burned alive. What was left was a melted figure. My heart sank.

I attempted to get closer, but it felt as if a supernatural force prevented me from going near him. It felt as if the presence of the Lord or an angelic being lingered in the room. I knew God at this point in my life, but I wasn't living for Him. I couldn't wrap my mind around what I was experiencing, but somehow, I knew it was God's presence in that room. A chill surged through my whole body. I stood there frozen. I felt like angels were protecting the soul of the child, ascending his spirit into Heaven. It was strange and terrifying at the same time. The impact of the situation was too much, making it hard for me to breathe.

Overcome with grief; I rushed outside. I gasped for a deep breath of cold air. I remember standing in the back of the house, staring up at the bright stars. A strange feeling came over me as if something from above was looking down at me. I felt so small in comparison. I couldn't stop thinking about the way the boy had died. I had questions, and nothing made sense in my mind. Was he afraid? Was he in pain? I couldn't help but think of my own small children. I stood there, stunned, trying to catch my breath. Yes, I was a cop, but I was a father too. Alone under the night sky, I cried for the little boy.

It bothered me for many days. The image of the boy kneeling by his bed replayed over and over in my mind. I couldn't stop visualizing the body of the child. It was an odd experience. Even with the emotional turmoil afterward, I was overcome with a sense of assurance that God's angels had ushered the boy into the spiritual realm. It was a feeling of peace. I couldn't help but wonder if I should have told the boy's father how we found him. I don't know if it would have helped. I could only hope that God had given him that same sense of peace He had provided for me.

As an adult, I have heard the phrase "child-like faith." Reflecting on this incident, I can see that expression was in action that night. That boy faced the scariest moment of his life, yet he spent those last moments praying to his heavenly father. He had an unwavering faith in God's love. I believe with all my heart that God was with that boy in his last moments. Now he's in Heaven and will never experience any more pain.

Several days later, I came across the story in the local newspaper. Arson investigators had concluded a lit candle had ignited the fire. The other son, a thirteen-year-old boy, died at the hospital due to smoke inhalation and other injuries sustained; two children passed away that night. A family was ripped apart and forever changed. It makes you think about how fragile life is and how things can change in an instant. I hugged my kids tight and thanked God for them being in my life. Don't take anything for granted. You never know when you've said your last goodbye.

Un-Faithful

After being on the force for several years, I began to work side-jobs while off duty. At the time, I had been married to Frances for more than five years. I started to notice that the uniform attracted many women. I believe that triggered the temptation I had for women to reignite. But I don't blame it all on the uniform. It was a problem I had for a while. While working security at nightclubs, pool halls, and beer joints, the challenge to stay loyal increased as I strayed away from God.

Reflecting on when I was a cadet, I remember an instructor saying something like, *the badge can attract a lot of women, but it only takes one to take that badge away.* In other words, you could lose your job over a woman!

There were occasions when I took off from work early to focus on other pleasures. Meanwhile, as my loyal wife was at home taking care of the kids, she became very suspicious that I was fooling around. She once told me, "One day Albert, in black and white, I'll find out the truth." When Frances said it, I was unsure what she meant by in black and white, and I thought about that for a good while. She was still faithfully attending church as I had lost interest. She continued to care for our children and pray for me. Yet, I cheated behind her back with several women.

A year had gone by, and my addiction to womanizing had become incredibly hard for me to stop. I'm not sure I even wanted to. Eventually, Frances caught me in a web of deceit. She discovered and confronted me with a copy of my scheduled time off from work. In black and white, official papers showed how I had been burning time from work without her being aware.

You may be wondering about the amount of disappointment my family had towards me. How could I be so cruel to a good wife? There were many times I hated myself for what I had done (this became a familiar pattern in my life). My self-centered pleasures had me entangled in adultery; there was no turning back.

Frances and I tried working things out. We followed up with marriage counseling. Moreover, Frances even called a well-known television evangelist in a desperate attempt to save our marriage. However, months later, I chose to leave Frances to follow my sinful ways.

24

Natasha

As I continued to follow my heart's desires, I met an attractive young waitress who waited on my partner and me. It was a well-known restaurant where officers would go to eat while on duty. It started as a casual conversation. At the time, I was still married to Frances. After several occasions at the eatery, I decided to ask the young lady for her name. She told us her name was Natasha. My partner and I listened as she explained that the restaurant was her second job, and her day job was working as a dental assistant. I didn't think that I had a chance with her.

On another occasion, while my partner and I were at the restaurant, I asked Natasha if she had ever considered a law enforcement career. In a previous conversation, she told us that working for the dentist was a bit boring. I explained that the department had a citizen ride-along program if she was interested. She said that it might be exciting to experience it. I told her that she could do the ride-along with either my partner or with me. She chose to ride with me.

After Natasha went on the ride-along program, we became friends. There was an age difference between us, she was twenty, and I was thirty-six. Although I was a married man, I became very attracted to her. I showed up at her day job unannounced. I pursued her and charmed her into liking me. The relationship didn't start right away, but eventually, the attraction became overwhelming for both of us. And gradually, we started falling in love.

By this time, Frances had finally lost all hope in me and divorced me after seven years of marriage. With much regret on my part, I had broken both Frances' and the children's hearts; and hurting them would haunt me for years to come.

Almost a year later, Natasha and I were married. I wanted to do well in this new marriage. We started attending church, which was another fresh start for me. A year and eight months after being married, our son Anthony was born. Things were going well in this new marriage. However, months later, tragedy would mark our lives.

My dad and me In Elgin, Illinois while 6 years old

On break at a cantina in Houston, Texas at the age of 15

1st time
Cadet Garcia
in 1984

On the force
in 1992

My firstborn son, John Michael Garcia, with his
Uncle Hector as Santa

My partner Johnny
and me

My mother Irma and me

At my retirement party with my kids and grand kids

My wife, Natasha and me

My siblings and I with our mom

25

The Accident

Tragically, on March 17, 1997, seven months after my son's birth, my ex-wife Frances lost her life in a car accident. I received the phone call from my stepdaughter, Jennifer, with the horrific news. I clearly remember slamming my fist on the wall as she was crying out. While hearing Jennifer weep on the phone, I couldn't believe it. Along with being tragic, it was so sudden. Frances was only 39 years old. Although the accident wasn't my fault, I felt such anger towards myself. I shamefully wondered if perhaps we hadn't divorced, maybe things would have turned out differently.

Three weeks before Frances' death, I had spoken with her on the phone about my son Albert. During the conversation, I felt an urgent need to apologize for causing her so much pain. For some reason, I knew that I had to tell her how sorry I was. She responded by saying, *"Albert, I have forgiven you."* Frances had a kind spirit, and it wasn't in her to live with un-forgiveness. She forgave me that day, and for that, I am genuinely grateful.

After Frances' funeral, my son Albert came home to live with me. Some of his mom's family members had wished that Albert could have stayed with his sisters. But he was my son, and I knew without a doubt that he belonged with me. Throughout the years, he visited with his sisters often. Albert became quite attached to his baby brother, Anthony. He had someone to take care of, which helped him deal with his mother's loss.

Frances was a good Christian woman who loved the Lord and loved her kids. After her death, I felt a lot of guilt and wondered if God was angry with me. It bothered me when I reminisced about her because my walk with God wasn't right!

Kingwood Division

In the latter part of 1996, Kingwood was annexed by the city of Houston. The result of the annexation led to the Houston Police Department abiding over the jurisdictions of Kingwood. Kingwood, which was also known as the Livable Forest, was just 25 miles north of downtown. It was considered an officer's retirement beat. That just meant the cops on patrol there typically had smoother shifts than the big-city officers. There was a low crime rate compared to the inner-city districts. Many of the residents weren't happy about being part of the metropolitan area, and who could blame them.

Several of my police buddies were assigned to the Livable Forest. They kept suggesting that I should consider going to work up there. By this time, I was married to Natasha, with my son Albert and an infant son, Anthony. My wife was also pregnant with our son, Andrew. I had nine years on the force. After a long thought-out decision, I chose to transfer to the Kingwood Division. A few months later, my son Andrew was born.

While patrolling the streets of Kingwood, I remember enjoying the views of the water on Lake Houston. I also enjoyed seeing the majestic trees, the green belt trails for jogging, and the occasional deer sighting. Most of the calls were of low priority, such as disturbances with disgruntled residents upset about a neighbor's dog running loose.

On slow evenings, I would initiate traffic enforcement and write a few tickets to show productivity. However, I was never one who enjoyed issuing tickets. *It was never my cup of tea u*nless the person was well deserving of it, and then it came with a stern lecture. For example, when the high school students got out of school, the youngsters would drag race down Kingwood Drive, making it a straightforward traffic citation.

After weeks of patrolling in Kingwood, I began to get a bit bored. I missed the action that surrounded *The Rock*. Nonetheless, I did enjoy working with my fellow officers, and it was less pressure there. Yet, I still reflected on why I wanted to be a cop. *And it was to fight crime!*

I quickly began noticing that the Livable Forest was not exempt from violent crimes. From time to time, a wave of robberies and burglaries would hit the region. Instinctively, I became excited about solving cases and apprehending suspects. I learned the most valuable investigative tool for solving these cases was the security camera!

From May to July of 1999, Kingwood and the Montgomery County area had a string of convenience store robberies. Three of the robberies occurred in my beat, which I did not take lightly; two other robberies occurred in Montgomery County. Most often, criminals were outsiders from jurisdictions like Atascocita, Montgomery County, and the Humble area. However, in this particular case, these individuals were actually from Kingwood.

After the robberies occurred, I requested approval from my Sergeant and HPD Robbery Division to work the Kingwood cases. Not long after, I linked the robbers in Montgomery to the same individuals committing the Kingwood robberies. Oddly, the suspects involved were young girls, wearing masks and brandishing a firearm. Notoriously, they called themselves the Queens of Armed Robbery!

Soon after, with a little legwork, I obtained a security video from another jurisdiction, which was later used for voice recognition by robbery investigators. One of the masked girls was identified from this video. The 17-year-old female confessed to the robberies and ratted out three other female accomplices. At the trial, all four girls were found guilty. And here I thought Kingwood was getting boring!

Ironically, the movie industry produced a comedy about the girls. Local news stations covered the story for days. National news outlets 20/20 and 48 Hours also did televised crime stories on the girls.

While assigned to the Kingwood substation, I got to work with outstanding sergeants who made sure the locals in the community felt safe. If it was not for them allowing a street cop to follow up on a hunch in locating perpetrators, many serious offenses could have gone unsolved. At the time, the Kingwood substation did not have an investigative unit, so most supervisors welcomed an officer's initiative to investigate possible leads. I commend those supervisors for their professionalism and the confidence they had in their subordinates.

Hebrews 12:5-7 (NIV)

*And have you completely
forgotten this word of
encouragement that addresses
you as a father addresses
his son? It says,"My son, do
not make light of the Lord's
discipline, and do not lose heart
when he rebukes you, because
the Lord disciplines the one he
loves, and he chastens everyone
he accepts as his son." Endure
hardship as discipline; God is
treating you as his children.
For what children are not
disciplined by their father?*

27

Broken

Some moments are fixed in your memory; these memories sometimes comfort you, sometimes they convict you, and sometimes they haunt you. For me, that moment came on January 27, 2001. It saddens me when I think back to that day. So much has changed since then. That was the day my world turned upside down. I became all too aware that officers and their families are not exempt from tragedies.

It was a Saturday afternoon, and I was looking forward to my shift because it was my Friday. My regular days off were Sundays and Mondays. As a police officer, you don't get a lot of time to spend with your family. When you're at work, you are entirely engaged in the task at hand because if you're not, it could be the difference between life and death. Your time off is precious because it might be another five days before you would spend any meaningful time with your family. I was looking forward to the coming Sunday; we planned to go to church and have lunch together.

As I walked into the station, I remember being in a joyful mood. It was a beautiful, cool crisp January day. I went straight to the roll call room, where all the officers were gathered. The atmosphere was buzzing, as everyone seemed to be ready to head out to the streets. The evening shift was usually the most active. I worked with some great officers in Kingwood, men I knew I could trust to have my back.

I hadn't been at the station long before the evening Sergeant waved me into his office. It was unusual but not worrisome. I assumed it wasn't anything serious, that maybe I needed to sign some paperwork. Once in his office, he asked me to take a seat, and I jokingly said, *"Is someone complaining about me? That's ok; I don't need to sit. What's up, Sarge?"* I could see it in his face and hear it in his voice; he was not joking. He was serious. He stood up to close the door behind me. His expression told me that it might not be good, so when he motioned to the chair and said, *"Have a seat,"* I did as he asked.

He looked me directly in the eyes and asked, "Do you have a son named John Michael Garcia?" Even though Michael had never been in trouble with the law, I immediately thought that he might've been arrested and assumed that was the reason for the Sergeant's mood. I nodded that I did and waited for him to tell me from which jail to fetch my son. But he didn't say anything like that. Instead, he said words that will haunt me all of my days.

"Garcia, Homicide Division has asked you to call them. They've found a body, and they think it might be your son. Are you alright?" It's hard to explain how I felt at that moment. My first instinct was to think he was joking, *even though that would've been a terrible joke to play on someone.* As the words left his mouth, I couldn't believe that they were right. I felt as if I were in a horrible nightmare, a haze enclosing me in his office, cutting me off from reality. I can't say how long I stayed in the seat. I sat there hoping it wasn't true, but deep down, I felt that it was. I knew that I'd want to be alone to make that phone call. I sensed that possibly it was Michael, and I did not want to be at the station when I made the call.

I told my Sergeant that I was going home and that I would call Homicide Division from there. I left his office and walked through the hallway, past the roll call room. Some read the grief on my face and asked if I was all right. I must have been stunned. I just kept walking past them; I mumbled that Homicide Division believed they had found my son's body. You can imagine how they felt—shocked perhaps, maybe sympathetic. I'm not too sure. I have to imagine it along with you because I can't recall. I was still in a haze, praying to God that I could wake up from this nightmare. They offered to drive me home, but I declined their offer because I wanted to be alone.

Once I was alone in my car, reality set in. I cried the whole way home. I had a terrible feeling. Homicide Division had identified a body; they simply suspected it might be my oldest boy, my firstborn son. There was still reason to hope. But I knew, deep down, I just knew. With each mile that brought me closer to home, the tears fell in abundance. I remembered the last time I'd seen Michael and spoken to him. It was just a few days earlier. He had stopped by the house. I remembered that as he was walking away, he stopped and turned to face me. It was as if time had stood still; his last words to me were, *"I love you, Dad."* And I said to him, *"I love you too, Son."* I remembered watching him walk away, and even though at the time I didn't know it, that was the last time I would see him alive. I know that God allowed us to have that moment.

When I walked into the house, I went straight to the phone to call homicide. I didn't bother to take my uniform or gun belt off. None of that mattered. The only thing that mattered was to find out about my son.

They asked if I had a son named John Michael Garcia, and I replied that I did. Next, they asked if I would go to the morgue and identify if the body was my son. The thought of waiting through Houston traffic while wondering if my son was dead was too much. I just needed to know. So I asked him a question: *"Can you give me a description of the deceased?"* They agreed and asked, *"Does your son have a dragon tattooed on the left side of his chest, accompanied by another tattoo of Asian writing?"* My heart sank, my mind began to spin, my stomach felt nauseous. It was my son. He was lying in the morgue, waiting for someone to claim him. I replied, *"Yes, that is my son; I don't need to go to the morgue."* I didn't want to see my son there. The grief was too overwhelming.

In my mind, I began investigating my son's death. My police instincts kicked in, along with anger. I asked the homicide investigator w*hat happened.* He informed me that the previous night, they had received a tip that there was a deceased person inside a car behind a movie theater. After the call came in, the police dispatcher sent a police unit to the theater to follow up and attempt to confirm the information. When the officer arrived, he confirmed that the person was, in fact, deceased. The detective advised me that they recovered my son's wallet, and that inside was a police business card, which had my name on it.

When I got off the phone, I cried out in anguish. I could not believe it. I couldn't wake up from this nightmare. Upon entering my bedroom, I began crying and screaming out to God, *"Why my son, Lord... why my son?"* In that instant, my thoughts began replaying past convictions. It was as if a home movie was playing, and it raced through my conscience. I already knew about God. But along the way, I betrayed so many people that loved me. With conviction, I dropped to my knees; I cried out to God with all my heart. Over and over, I told the Lord how sorry I was. I repeatedly asked Him to forgive me. I cried out, *"Lord, I am so sorry for all the sins that I have committed. Lord, please forgive me for all the things I have done wrong. I'm tired of doing things on my own. I've made a mess on my own. Lord, please take control of my life, and help me. I need you, Lord. I can't do this on my own any longer."* I meant every word I spoke with my whole heart. I needed Him.

Romans 10:9 (NIV) That if you confess with your mouth, "Jesus is Lord," and believe in your heart that God raised him from the dead, you will be saved.

I had turned my back on God. It was as if He was a distant memory even after all he did for me! But, here I was, calling on Him again! In those moments, God had my full attention. It was then that I truly gave my heart to Jesus. It was then that God changed me; Jesus came into my heart. It was different this time. The first time I had given my life to Jesus, I said it with my mouth. This time I meant it from the heart. He came in and cleansed me from my sins. He can do the very same for you. All you have to do is ask Him.

Then reality settled in; I needed to make the call to give my son's mother the horrifying news. I didn't know how to tell her that our son was no longer alive. I asked God to provide me with the strength, and I made the call. It was the worst phone call I've ever had to make.

Even though my spirit was broken, I did not blame God for Michael's death. But, I did think it was strange that my ex-wife Frances happened to die on the same day that my son Michael was born. I often wondered if this was a coincidence or if it occurred for a deeper reason. I thought it was a divine reminder. They were both gone. Honestly, at the time, I felt that God used my son's death to discipline me for my past disobedience. It felt like the wrath of God had come down on me. I didn't think that God had caused his death, but I believe he used it to change me.

The week before Michael's death, I had an opportunity to be with another woman, re-triggering my lustful temptations. Although nothing had occurred, it was in the making. God knew my intentions. He knew I was about to entangle myself in another adulterous situation. I was faithfully devoted to Natasha for five years, but I was getting ready to fall back into the pit of adultery. I believe God foresaw another broken home with yet another loyal wife. My heart was not right in God's eyes, and it needed to be broken. Sadly, it took my son's death for me to realize that.

I'm not saying that my son or Frances' death was a good thing, but the chances are that my heart would not have changed if they had not died.

God gives us a choice to choose which road we are going to take. Seemingly, I was going down the wrong path in my life. God knew I needed to change for the good. I had to admit that I had a sin issue for the healing process to begin. It was about His salvation.

Psalms 105:3 (NIV) Glory in his holy name; let the hearts of those who seek the Lord rejoice.

Thank you, JESUS, for forgiving me!

Two months after losing Michael, the investigative report would confirm that his death was an accident. Michael accidentally shot himself. The gun belonged to a homeowner who was on probation for a pistol case. Since it was a violation for him to own a firearm, he panicked and ordered his friends to get rid of the body. They would leave my son's lifeless body in his car, behind a local movie theater, where the police later found him. The individuals who moved Michael's body went to jail for tampering with evidence and moving a body.

Many emotions were going through my mind in the weeks that followed Michael's burial. The investigation was still ongoing, and there were many nights that I wavered between wondering if it was an accident or if my son was murdered. The debate in my mind went back and forth from one to the other. I would often pray to God, asking Him to give me a sign that Michael's death was an accident.

Michael's friends who were present when the incident occurred showed up at the funeral. After the eulogy concluded, I pulled one of them to the side to ask him what had happened. He explained that Michael was messing with the gun when there was a malfunction, and the magazine fell out. He was unaware that the gun had one round left in the chamber. The friend's account of the shooting collaborated with the statements obtained from the detectives. Even after I found this out, I still doubted.

It just hurt too much, and I didn't know what to believe.

I couldn't bear to drive-by the movie theater where they left my son's body inside of his car. Night and day, I prayed for God to send me a sign. But His timing is not our timing. God's timing is always right on time. He knew I couldn't bear another day without knowing the truth.

I remember every detail about the moment that God answered my prayer. I was driving and had just exited the toll road to merge onto Highway 249. For some reason, I forgot that I would have to pass the area where they left Michael. I couldn't get off the highway, so I had no choice but to continue. Twilight was beginning, but there was an ample amount of light in the sky, and it was clear as could be. I was in deep thought about Michael as I was praying to God. Simultaneously, I saw a bright star shoot across the sky. That beautiful star shined right before my eyes just as I passed the area where Michael was left.

At that moment, I felt the Holy Spirit comfort me.

That evening the Lord had given me a sign; something that was for me and me alone. The Lord assured me that night that Michael's death was an accident.

I would finally put the question that bothered me so much to rest.

The Power of Prayer

I didn't go back to work until a month after my son's death. It was a hard time in my life. When I did return to work, I began to have a close relationship with the Lord. The Holy Spirit began to guide me in every area of my life, especially in my job. I went back to patrolling my beat in Kingwood. I was still solving robberies, which was very encouraging. It was exciting to outsmart the crooks; it gave me an adrenaline rush. I started praying for investigative leads, and God began providing the clues.

The following are just a few examples of where God answered my prayers on critical cases:

Robbery Suspect Arrested

One day on my way to work, I asked God for a lead on a robber wanted for two counts. I was in my personal car at the intersection of Northpark and Woodland Hills, when lo and behold, I recognized the suspect from a security video that I had reviewed. Not having a police radio with me, I called the roll call sergeant to send me a marked police unit as I kept an eye on the male. Unsurprisingly, half of the shift showed up! The suspect was immediately apprehended and later positively identified from a photo spread. That same day, a young officer asked me, "How do you find these guys?" I laughed and responded, "If I tell you, you probably won't believe me." He looked puzzled, at which I said, *"I pray to God to help me find the suspects!"* He just smiled in amazement.

Toy Store Robbery

An aggravated robbery occurred at a local toy store in Kingwood. A suspect robbed a female cashier at gunpoint while making threatening remarks. During the robbery, the suspect stole the victim's cell phone, which turned out to be crucial to the investigation. Both Officer Johnny and I were determined to find this suspect. So we followed up on the case. The suspect was dumb enough to use the stolen phone to make calls. Through the victim's phone records, we discovered that the suspect made calls to California. That's how we were able to determine who committed the robbery. The victim positively identified the suspect from a constructed photo spread. We filed charges against the robber, and a warrant was issued for his arrest. However, the suspect had fled to California, and the authorities there were having trouble finding our suspect. I prayed that God would allow the suspect to be apprehended. I asked my wife to pray along with me. Soon after praying, the suspect was found and arrested and later extradited to Texas.

My First Informant

There was an armed robbery, where three young Hispanic males roughed-up the owner of a store. I figured I would look into the case because the suspects spoke only Spanish while committing the crime. Since I also spoke Spanish, I requested clearance from Robbery Division to work the case. As I had done many times before, I prayed for God to guide me to the right people. During the investigation, I was able to get a lead from a cooperating citizen; coincidentally, this citizen turned out to have a wealth of information on high-profile gang members operating across the Houston area. This reliable source would later help to solve several violent crimes, including murder. He corroborated that the three robbery suspects were part of the same gang. The individual became my first official informant. Thankfully, with God's guidance, I was able to solve the case.

I marveled at how God gradually revealed himself to me as I talked and prayed to Him more and more! I was delighted to see what was occurring in my walk with God. He was listening and answering my prayers according to His will.

1 John 5:14 (NIV) This is the confidence we have in approaching God: that if we ask anything according to his will, he hears us.

The Comfort Zone

I was genuinely enjoying solving robberies in Kingwood, but I had a new supervisor who disapproved of patrolmen doing detective work. He believed that it was the job of the detectives to solve the investigations. I started to sense that God wanted me to leave Kingwood, the problem being I was comfortable there. Disappointment settled in as I felt like the Lieutenant was running me off. It was time to leave The Livable Forest. It was time to get out of my comfort zone. Therefore, I decided to transfer. Looking back, I learned that with God, when one door closes, another one opens.

I remember the first day I reported to the North Patrol Station, *from the suburb to the ghetto*. While in the roll call room, a few officers asked me, "What station did you transfer from?" I told them that I came from Kingwood patrol. They laughed as they said, "What are you doing in this hell hole?" I told them it was a long story, as I smiled. Yep, I was back in the hood working the afternoon shift, patrolling Airline Drive and the Crosstimbers area. *I thought to myself, so much for the emerald green scenery.* Narcotics and prostitution were the new scenery in my beat.

North Patrol Station was a high crime area in the inner city. I ran service calls as a one-man unit. Once there, I interviewed for a tactical team position; however, I didn't get selected. My morale would be low at this point in my career. I had just left a place that I loved, and now I was patrolling rough streets. I wouldn't be there for long, though. God's favor was right around the corner.

Gang Division

30

Two months after arriving at the North Station, I received a phone call out of the blue. On the other end was a sergeant from Gang Division. As I listened attentively, I couldn't believe what I was hearing. The sergeant stated, "Garcia, you have an assignment to report to Gang Division for ninety days. You will report Monday morning to 1200 Travis (headquarters), and you can't refuse. You will be working in plain clothes and you'll have a take-home car. You will have Saturdays and Sundays off with plenty of overtime." As I listened in amazement, I was almost speechless and responded, *"Yes, sir!"* Sarcastically, I thought to myself, how could I deny an assignment like that? I knew God was working in my life. I always believed that I would end my career as a patrol cop, proudly wearing the blue uniform. But God had other plans!

At the time, Houston was having a citywide problem with high-profile crimes such as murders, robberies, and narcotics trafficking that involved gangs. The Gang Division implemented an initiative to disrupt and dismantle violent gangs. This operation would consist of a multi-agency task force.

God was getting ready to show me a different level of crime-fighting, both spiritually and mentally.

When Monday morning came around, I was sitting at headquarters in a large conference room, surrounded by many of the department's elite investigators. I knew that God had plans for me, but I almost felt embarrassed to say that I came from patrol as I stood to introduce myself. I felt under-qualified to be sitting there. I had over 17 years in the department, all of them being on the streets. I wondered if the investigators probably thought to themselves, *"What is he doing here?"* However, I had confidence that I could get the job done, especially with God on my side.

After several months of working in gangs, a permanent position opened up. My new title became Al Garcia, Gang Investigator. While working in Gang Division, I had the honor of working with some of the department's top investigators in a combined effort with outside agencies. Most cases consisted of a team effort. While working in Investigations, one of the assignments was to assist the Homicide and Robbery Division by locating fugitive gang members, and this was right up my alley!

Here are a few cases we worked in gangs:

The Idol

While working on many gangs and narcotics trafficking assignments, I noticed a distinctive tattoo that many Hispanic gang members had. The tattoo was of La Santa Muerte (the holy mother of death), also known as La Flaca. According to the information I gathered from interviews, the image is considered a religious idol. Many members proclaim their faith in her. They believe that praying to her will lead to blessings and wealth in their criminal operations.

I saw firsthand the painful, spiritual destruction that this curse brought to the families who worshipped this idol. God began to show me that the principalities of darkness were operating within them.

The gang members would worship and even pray to La Santa Muerte, but they prayed to the wrong entity. I believe this was the reason that destruction often came upon them.

One day on a follow-up investigation, I was interviewing a cooperating gang member. He explained that a rival gang killed his brother in a drive-by shooting. He sadly described the details of his brother's death as he shared his story concerning La Santa Muerte. He said that a few weeks before getting killed, his brother got a tattoo on his chest of the idol. He believed it was strange and that it might have brought bad luck to his brother.

At a separate incident, our squad executed an arrest warrant for organized crime at a home where the suspect had a three-foot-tall ceramic statue of La Santa Muerte. There was fruit surrounding the idol, with incense burning. Concerned, I felt the Lord tell me to let the man know about the destruction worshipping the idol would bring. I asked the man in Spanish if he believed in God. He looked at me and was startled that I had asked him that. He responded, *"Yes, I believe in God!"* I replied, *"Well, you know God is a jealous God, and if the idol in the back room worked, then we wouldn't be here right now!"*

There were occasions where I tried to tell gang members the negative aspects of being in a gang. I told them the trouble that comes from worshipping the idol. And I also would speak to them about God. Sadly, some were too hard-core and didn't care to hear about Him. The younger ones were prone to listen with an open mind; however, the older ones were not.

Hand's Up

Many of my leads came from reviewing old offense reports and researching the criminal history of gang members. These records were crucial to an investigation by helping to locate acquaintances of the suspects. And as usual, God would lead me to the right reports and the cooperating sources. It always inspired me to go out and apprehend the suspects. God was guiding me!

Most of the helpful information came from Spanish-speaking individuals in the Hispanic community. Just the mention of receiving money from crime-stoppers would usually get their attention, along with the fact that they wanted the gang members removed from their communities.

On a case I was working, a Homicide detective requested assistance in locating two gang members who were wanted for capital murder. After interviewing several acquaintances, I received a tip from someone acknowledging the suspects' hideout location with a detailed description of their vehicle.

I immediately contacted my sergeant to fill him in on the possible lead. Next, I reached out to two uniform officers assigned to our division. I provided them with the details of the suspects' likely whereabouts. I directed them to follow up on a location and inform me if the car was still there. Several minutes later, I received confirmation that the suspects' car was parked at the apartment complex.

After a safety briefing with our team and other police units, we headed to the apartment to execute the arrest. The suspects' apartment was an upstairs unit. As we knocked at the front door, a citizen quickly informed us that two males had jumped out a second-story window. The suspects' were on the run.

Our team quickly jumped in their patrol cars and scattered in the area, searching the vicinity for the suspects.

I jumped in my undercover vehicle and drove around to the south side of the apartment complex. Did I mention I was in plain clothes? When I spotted the two males with tattoos standing suspiciously on the other side of the apartment's wooden fence, I immediately reacted.

Right away, I put out a radio transmission on my portable radio, informing my backup of the suspects' location. There was no time to wait for my team to show up; I had to act quickly. My adrenaline was in over-drive. I jumped out of my car and yelled, *"Police, get on the ground now!"*

One suspect ran northbound as I held the other suspect at gunpoint! Citizens were watching this unfold in broad daylight and called 911 about a man and a gun. Before I knew it, police cars were racing through the parking lot. In my head, I was relieved to think my backup had finally arrived. However, the next thing I knew, the cops were pointing their guns and yelling at both of us. They screamed, *"Put your hands up now!"*

"I am HPD!" I yelled back.

"Let me see your ID" screamed the officers! In my haste to jump out and apprehend the suspects, I realized that I had left it in my vehicle. *Oh boy*, I had just become the suspect of their 911 call.

After the situation calmed down and the police officers realized I was indeed HPD, my marked unit informed them that we were executing a warrant. As I glanced over to my unit's patrol car, I saw that they had the suspect that took off running already in the back seat. By this time, I realized that my police radio battery had died. This explained why the policemen from that district were oblivious to who I was, since the transmission I put out never went through.

Looking back at the situation, I laugh with my wife, who thought it was hilarious. However, it wasn't too funny at the time. Thank God no one was hurt in the incident, only my pride.

A couple of our team members were all jokes about it. One jokester even drew a comical sketch where my hands were up. All jokes aside, two violent gang members were taken off the streets that day.

The Fugitive

Two Immigration and Custom Enforcement (ICE) agents requested HPD Gang investigators' assistance to locate and capture a documented gang member. The gang member was wanted for murdering two elderly American tourists in Mexico during a robbery. According to the agents, they believed the killer had made his way back to Houston by using the money that belonged to the victims. The suspect had previously lived in Houston before being deported back to Mexico.

After developing a probable lead from the Harris County criminal database, I located an old assault report. In it, I noticed that a suspect had used a knife on a Houston area resident. This suspect also had an outstanding warrant for assault. He had a different last name than what the agents had given me, but the DOB was the same. I wondered if this was the same individual who killed the Americans. Even though the last names were different, the information still appeared promising. I advised my partner to saddle-up because we might have a good lead.

After my partner and I interviewed the victim from the Houston case, we discovered that we were on the right trail. The victim provided information where the suspect was known to hang out and identified a photo of the individual wanted by ICE.

By this time, the U.S. Marshalls were also briefed, and we were out doing surveillance, hoping to make an arrest. Within a few hours, while my partner and I were staking out a location, we identified the suspect walking to a car with a female companion. *The Jig was up!*

We began rolling Northbound. We radioed for a patrol unit to be ready to make a felony stop when the suspect's vehicle came to the stop sign! We arrested the gang member without resistance. Upon searching beneath the gang member's seat, we discovered a large kitchen knife. We advised dispatch that we had one in custody! All the glory goes to God, for he had come through again.

Most officers want justice for the victims of heinous crimes. Imagine your son was robbed and beaten while jogging or your daughter was raped while leaving work; as a parent, you would want the criminal to be caught and tried in court for what they did to your loved one. What motivated me every day was the desire to see justice served for the victims and their families.

There are some investigations where detectives are not able to bring the offenders to justice. Some investigators retire with that one unsolvable case. I had a similar case, which caused many nagging thoughts and sleepless nights. I prayed for many years that I would find two individuals wanted for the murder of a young man, to no avail. I desperately wanted to see the family get justice for the death of their son. My wife once told me, "Albert, maybe it's not God's will that you find these individuals yet? In His timing, they will get caught; if not, they will have justice from God!" Even though it bothered me, I never let it stop me from doing God's work.

I genuinely believe that being a police officer is a calling from God. And there's a reason God calls men and women to this profession. His Word says that he establishes all authority. I worked with many dedicated officers who went above and beyond the call of duty to ensure justice was served. God's Word talks about law enforcement officers in Romans.

> Evil prospers, where good men do nothing
>
> —John Philpot Curran.

Romans 13:1-5 (NIV)

1) Everyone must SUBMIT to the governing authorities, for there is no authority except that which God has established. The authorities that exist have been established by God. 2) Consequently, he who rebels against the authority is rebelling against what God has instituted, and those who do so will bring judgment on themselves. 3) For rulers hold no terror for those who do right, but for those who do wrong. Do you want to be free from fear of the one in authority? Then do what is right, and he will commend you. 4) For he is God's servant to do you good. But if you do wrong, be afraid, for he does not bear the sword for nothing. He is God's servant, an agent of wrath to bring punishment on the wrongdoer. 5) Therefore, it is necessary to SUBMIT to the authorities, not only because of possible punishment but also because of conscience.

31

In God We Trust

During my first two years in Gang Division, my faith in God was the strongest it had ever been. I would meditate on the word of God in the mornings before going to work. My prayer life became more profound as I became more obedient to God. I prayed for many things, but my heart's resounding cry was never to lose another child. Every day was a work in progress, but wholeheartedly I was willing to accept God's way. I wasn't turning back to the prideful man I was before. My intimate walk with God led me down a path to where He gave me tangible signs.

One day, as I quietly sat in my city ride, praying for a clue on a case, I stepped out, and on the ground, a penny caught my attention. At first glance, I thought maybe it was a sign of luck, so I picked it up and placed it in my pocket. This would later become a mysterious reoccurrence. I would pray and ask the Lord for leads in my cases, and soon after, I would find pennies. Every time a penny appeared, it was as if God was telling me that I was on the right track. His Holy

Spirit was undoubtedly guiding me. What I thought to be luck at first glance was not luck at all. It was a mystery, and I felt it was God's way of communicating with me.

I joyfully marvel at the mystery of the pennies that God would reveal to me. As time went on, it even seemed like the pennies were finding me. It became so meaningful to me that I began collecting them throughout my time in gang division. I would place those precious copper coins in a jar. Soon after that, one jar became two, and two jars became three. It was just a simple penny, but it reminded me of what is written on the coin, "In God We Trust!"

Each penny that I retrieved was different from the last. Some pennies were shiny and new. Some were scratched and dull. Some were dirty, and one was broken, with only three-fourths of the coin left. Pennies have been run over, rained on, and abandoned. God showed me that people's lives are much like the penny; some people lead comfortable lives, some struggle, and some are rundown and beat up. Finding pennies became a reason to trust that God would direct me along my path.

Psalms 25:5 (NIV)

Guide me in your truth and teach me; for you are God my Savior, and my hope is in you all day long.

Coincidence

Many people might wonder if God knows what happens in our future, or is it just a coincidence? The dictionary says that a coincidence is a remarkable concurrence of circumstance without an apparent connection. Are there reasons for the things we experience in this life? Reflecting back, it was evident that God works in mysterious ways. I pondered on this many times while writing this story about my relationship with the Lord! Could my circumstances have been a coincidence, or was it destiny? Was it a carefully sought-out plan constructed before I was even born?

Was it a coincidence that God used a cross on a necklace to draw me unto Him? Could it have been a coincidence that God would use a radio advertisement to ignite the desire in me to become a policeman? Could God have actually used pennies to let me know he was with me?

I think about Frances' losing her life on the same day as Michael's birthday. I often wonder if her and Michael's death happened for the reason that only God knew. I would go to their gravesite throughout the years, as they are buried in the same cemetery. I would occasionally take my younger sons, Anthony and Andrew, to the cemetery with me. On Michael's birthday, I would place flowers on his footstone. I would also stop by to pay my respects at Frances' gravesite. While putting flowers on her grave, my son Andrew, who was nine years old at the time, noticed her tombstone's date. He asked me, "Dad, she died on Michael's birthday?" I replied, "Yes, son, one day, I will tell you the story." Eventually, I told him what happened. It's such a mystery to me, and I will tell you it always makes me think.

I think that we use the word coincidence to explain that which we cannot explain. I believe that my experiences and my walk with God were not coincidences at all. For it is He who determines the outcome; God knows all things! God knew us before we were born. But the choices we make are up to us. And because God loves us, he is merciful enough to forgive us for the bad decisions we make. There's no offense too great that He can't forgive. No matter what we've done, God can turn it around.

Ephesians 1:11-12 (NIV)

In him we were also chosen, having been predestine according to the plan of him who works out everything in conformity with the purpose of his will, in order that we, who were the first to hope in Christ, might be for the praise of his glory.

God has definitely turned my life around. I have come a long way from playing in the band. I am no longer the adulterer I once was. God has forgiven and changed me. It's no longer about me; it's about my relationship with the Lord!

God has blessed me with a beautiful family. I am very grateful for the relationships I have with my children Brandi, Albert, Anthony, and Andrew; they are my blessings. I have unconditional love for each of my grandkids. I try my best to be a good Graspa and G-pa. By God's grace, my wife,

Natasha, has stood by my side. I have been faithful to her for twenty-six years. I thank her for all her love and loyalty to me.

I am human, and I do question each life lesson that I went through. They made me the person I am today. I know that He has been with me every step of the way. Years ago, I made a vow to God that I would tell my story. I would speak of God's goodness through the good and the bad.

Through it all, His love never failed! To God, I give all the glory! He is the hero in my story!

Therefore this is what the Lord says:

Jeremiah 16:19-20 (NIV)
"If you repent, I will restore you that you may serve me; if you utter worthy, not worthless, words, you will be my spokesman. Let this people turn to you. But you must not turn to them. I will make you a wall to this people, a fortified wall of bronze; they will fight against you but will not overcome you, for I am with you to rescue and save you."

33

Memory Lane

My last cherished memory as a police officer began on a beautiful, calm day in October. The weather was cool enough to wear long sleeves. The blue sky made the backdrop of Houston's skyline look very impressive. I was donating my scheduled time to guard The Houston Police Memorial located on Memorial Drive. It was such an honor to work at the monument. Some of the officers' who lost their lives in the line of duty were my friends.

I was in full uniform when I began reminiscing back to when I was a fifteen-year-old kid, playing along the Buffalo Bayou. The police monument had not been built yet. My childhood friends and I would ride our bikes there, and sometimes we would swim in the murky Bayou.

As I walked along the quiet asphalt trail that leads to the police memorial, I thought to myself about God's goodness. Throughout my life, His favor was always evident. Despite my wrong choices, His mercy never failed. The conviction and guilt I once had were gone. I felt His love all around. Between God and me, there was now a strong bond. We now had a relationship, one that I am forever grateful for.

I spent several minutes looking at the names inscribed on the monument; too many were recognizable. I started walking the trail back to the security shack. I began giving the Lord praises for giving me the desire to become a Houston Police officer. In that serene moment, a refreshing breeze brushed up against my body. The trees began to sway with the wind. It was as if God's breath was making the tree leaves applaud together in unison. I felt his presence with a soft touch on my spirit, reassuring me that he was pleased with what I had done with my life. Upon reaching the security shack, there on the ground was a penny. I knew HE was there with me, through it all!

Jeremiah 24:7 (NIV) *I will give them a heart to know me, that I am the Lord. They will be my people, and I will be their God, for they will return to me with all their heart.*

Made in USA - Kendallville, IN
62680_9780996631785
01.18.2022 1004